Independent Schools
Examinations Board

SCIENCE

ISEB Revision Guide

(2nd edition)

Richard Balding

Independent Schools
Examinations Board

www.galorepark.co.uk

GALORE PARK

Published by ISEB Publications, an imprint of Galore Park Publications Ltd
19/21 Sayers Lane, Tenterden, Kent TN30 6BW
www.galorepark.co.uk

Design and typesetting Typetechnique

Printed by Charlesworth Press

ISBN: 978 1 907047 69 5

First edition published 2009, second edition published 2011, 2012

Details of other ISEB Revision Guides for Common Entrance, examination
papers and Galore Park publications are available at www.galorepark.co.uk

Front cover photo of Clark's anemonefish in sea anemone, Indonesia
© David Fleetham/Alamy

About the author

Richard Balding has a wide experience of teaching science in prep schools, culminating in twenty-six years running the science department at Summer Fields. During his career, he has been the IAPS science co-ordinator, chairman of the Physics Common Entrance setting panel and SATIPS broadsheet editor, and was a marker for Key Stage 3 SATS. Publications include books on physics, chemistry and biology, written for prep schools. Now retired from teaching, he is active as an ISI inspector, writing and editing science books.

Contents

Introduction

This book is to help you to produce your best in the Common Entrance examination at 11+ and 13+. Apart from working carefully through your course, you will need to do some revision, especially as it may be two years since you studied some of the early topics. As this book is a revision guide, it only contains an outline of the topics that will be examined; fuller treatment of these will be found in *So you really want to learn Science* Books 1 and 2. To find out if you know and understand the key facts within each topic, a selection of sample questions is included in each section.

In the 13+ examination, questions will be set that will assume a thorough knowledge of the topics covered at 11+. It is always a good idea to read through the 11+ materials on the topic you are revising. As in most cases you will be refreshing what you know already, this will be a relatively small, but worthwhile, task.

Throughout the book you will see grey boxes containing different sorts of information. The symbols in the boxes tell you what the information is about: ⓘ important key facts; ⚗ important information about experiments; ✓ exam hints and revision tips.

The syllabus and your examinations

To help you in planning your revision, it is useful to know about the syllabus used for the exam.

This is revised regularly and is based on the programme of study for Key Stage 2 (11+) and Key Stage 3 (13+) of the National Curriculum. Because Key Stage 3 covers years 7–9, the Common Entrance syllabus does not include all Key Stage 3 topics; many of these will be taught at senior school level. The National Curriculum divides science into four attainment targets:

How science works (AT1): these are key concepts, skills and processes (listed below), which pupils need to experience to deepen and broaden their understanding of science and which complement the scientific content of the syllabus.

- **Scientific thinking**
  - (a) using scientific ideas and models to explain phenomena and developing them creatively to generate and test theories;
  - (b) analysing and evaluating evidence critically from observations and experiments;

- **Applications and implications of science**
  - (a) exploring how the creative application of scientific ideas can bring about technological developments and consequent changes in the way people think and behave;
  - (b) examining the ethical and moral implications of using and applying science;

- **Cultural understanding**

    (a) recognising that modern science has its roots in many different societies and cultures, and draws on a variety of valid approaches to scientific practice;

- **Collaboration**

    (a) sharing developments and common understanding across disciplines and boundaries;

- **Practical and enquiry skills**

    (a) using a range of scientific methods and techniques to develop and test ideas and explanations;

    (b) assessing risk and working safely in the laboratory, field and work place*;

    (c) planning and carrying out practical and investigative activities, both individually and in groups;

- **Critical understanding of evidence**

    (a) obtaining, recording and analysing data from a wide range of primary and secondary sources, including ICT sources, using their findings to provide evidence for scientific explanations;

    (b) evaluating scientific evidence and working methods;

- **Communication**

    (a) using appropriate methods, including ICT, to communicate scientific information and contribute to presentations and discussions about scientific issues.

Life processes and living things (AT2): the biology content of the course.

Materials and their properties (AT3): the chemistry content of the course.

Physical processes (AT4): the physics content of the course.

At 13+, it is expected that material in Key Stages 1 and 2 has already been fully covered and questions in the 13+ examination may well contain material covered by these two levels.

11+

At 11+, there is a single 60-minute paper, carrying 80 marks. The paper will test

- Organisms, their behaviour and the environment

- Materials, their properties and the Earth

- Energy, forces and space

with approximately equal weighting. Questions will be included to enable candidates to demonstrate their developing skills in **How science works**. Each paper may contain a question giving candidates the opportunity for free writing to a maximum of 4 marks.

There will be no choice of questions. The use of calculators will be allowed in the examination.

*Teachers should assess risk and pay due regard to safety when planning and supervising practical activities. CLEAPPS and the Association of Science Education are valued and trusted sources of important information.

13+ Assessment of the 13+ syllabus can occur at two levels: Level 1 and Level 2. The syllabus is common for both levels, although those parts of the syllabus which are underlined will only be assessed on Level 2 papers. It is envisaged that candidates who are expected to achieve less than an average of 40% on the three Level 2 papers should consider using the Level 1 paper.

Level 1 (80 marks; 60 minutes)
There will be one paper with approximately equal numbers of questions based on the 13+ biology, chemistry and physics syllabuses. The paper will consist of a mixture of closed items, e.g. multiple choice, matching pairs, completing sentences and some open questions. Open questions will have several parts, some of which will require answers of one or two sentences. These parts will carry a maximum of 2 marks. Up to 10% of the marks on the paper will be available for plotting graphs or making simple calculations, such as calculating means from data or using a formula.

There will be no choice of questions. The use of calculators and protractors will be allowed in the examination.

Level 2 (60 marks; 40 minutes)
There will be three papers, one in each of biology, chemistry and physics. Some of the questions may be closed, although most will be open with several parts requiring candidates to answer in sentences. These parts will carry a maximum of 3 marks. In addition, 1 mark may be given for an acceptable standard of spelling, punctuation and grammar in one part of the paper. The maximum number of marks per question will be 12. At least 25% of the paper will be testing 'How science works'?

There will be no choice of questions. The use of calculators and protractors will be allowed in the examination.

SCHOLARSHIP

Scholarship papers are based on this syllabus. The Common Academic Scholarship Examination (90 minutes, including 10 minutes' reading time) will be divided into three sections: A (Biology), B (Chemistry) and C (Physics). Each section will contain two questions. Candidates will be required to attempt three questions, one from each section. Each question will carry 20 marks. The use of calculators and protractors will be allowed in the examination.

Tips on revising

Get the best out of your brain

- Give your brain plenty of oxygen by exercising. You can revise effectively if you feel fit and well.

- Eat healthy food while you are revising. Your brain works better when you give it good fuel.

- Think positively. Give your brain positive messages so that it will want to study.

- Keep calm. If your brain is stressed it will not operate effectively.

- Take regular breaks during your study time.

- Get enough sleep. Your brain will carry on sorting out what you have revised while you sleep.

Get the most from your revision

- Don't work for hours without a break. Revise for 20–30 minutes then take a five-minute break.

- Do good things in your breaks: listen to your favourite music, eat healthy food, drink some water, do some exercise and juggle. Don't read a book, watch TV or play on the computer; it will conflict with what your brain is trying to learn.

- When you go back to your revision review what you have just learnt.

- Regularly review the facts you have learnt.

Get motivated

- Set yourself some goals and promise yourself a treat when the exams are over.

- Make the most of all the expertise and talent available to you at school and at home. If you don't understand something ask your teacher to explain.

- Get organised. Find a quiet place to revise and make sure you have all the equipment you need.

- Use year and weekly planners to help you organise your time so that you revise all subjects equally. (Available for download from www.galorepark.co.uk)

- Use topic and subject checklists to help you keep on top of what you are revising. (Available for download from www.galorepark.co.uk)

Know what to expect in the examination

- Use past papers to familiarise yourself with the format of the exam.

- Make sure you understand the language examiners use.

Before the examination

- Have all your equipment and pens ready the night before.

- Make sure you are at your best by getting a good night's sleep before the exam.

- Have a good breakfast in the morning.

- Take some water into the exam if you are allowed.

- Think positively and keep calm.

During the examination

- Have a watch on your desk. Work out how much time you need to allocate to each question and try to stick to it.

- Make sure you read and understand the instructions and rules on the front of the exam paper.

- Allow some time at the start to read and consider the questions carefully before writing anything.

- Read all the questions at least twice. Don't rush into answering before you have a chance to think about it.

- If a question is particularly hard move on to the next one. Go back to it if you have time at the end.

- Check your answers make sense if you have time at the end.

Tips for the science examination

- You should write your answers on the question paper; you may use a calculator and remember all questions should be attempted.

- Look at the number of marks allocated for each question, in order to assess how many relevant points are required for a full answer.

- Very often, marks are awarded for giving your reasons for writing a particular answer.

- In numerical questions, workings out should be shown and the correct units used.

- Practical skills are important. Look back in your lab notes to remind yourself about why you carried out any practical work. What were you trying to find out? What did you actually do? What instrument did you use to take any measurements and what units did you use? How did you record your results: tables, bar charts or graphs? What were the results of your investigation and did you make any plans to change or improve what you did? These are all important and will be tested in the examination.

- A thorough understanding of your practical work will also help you to remember the key facts by putting them into context.

- Neat handwriting and careful presentation may help to put the examiner in a more generous frame of mind!

For more tips on how to get the best from your revision and exams see *Study Skills* by Elizabeth Holtom, published by Galore Park.

Useful resources

Study Skills by Elizabeth Holtom, ISBN: 9781902984599

So you really want to learn Science Book 1 by WR Pickering,
ISBN: 9781902984216

So you really want to learn Science Book 1 Answer Book by WR Pickering,
ISBN: 9781905735099

So you really want to learn Science Book 2 by WR Pickering,
ISBN: 9781902984377

So you really want to learn Science Book 2 Answer Book by WR Pickering,
ISBN: 9781902984384

All available from Galore Park: www.galorepark.co.uk

BIOLOGY

Chapter 1: 11+ Biology

1.1 Life processes

What is a living thing?

A living thing is called an **organism**.

This term will apply to **any living thing** whether it is the smallest bacterium or the tallest tree.

Whilst there are huge numbers of different organisms, there will be processes that they carry out which are shared by each and every one of them in order that they may be classified as living. These are called **life processes**.

There are seven of these processes, but you are only required to know **four** of them at this stage.

1.   Nutrition

Just as car engines require fuel to make them work, so all organisms need to be able to obtain and absorb food which provides them with **energy** to live and **materials** to help build up and maintain their bodies.

- **Animals**: food needs to be broken down by the process called **digestion**, so that they can use the different types of chemicals in the food in various ways.

- **Plants**: the process is less obvious, but you will know that plants die if they are starved of water and that they need certain minerals to achieve healthy growth.

2.   Movement

- **Animals**: this is obvious as they will move from place to place to find food, or escape from being someone else's food. They will move to find a mate, shelter, or to escape natural disasters such as floods or forest fires.

- **Plants**: movement is so slow that it cannot be seen with the naked eye. Petals will open and close and whole flower heads will turn following the path of the sun. Shoots respond to light and roots to gravity. Even though they have moved, you will not have been able to detect the slow movement.

3.   Reproduction

- All organisms need to reproduce.

- As each individual organism, sooner or later, will die, it is vital that they are able to make more of their own kind so that there is **continuity** of that type of organism.

- This is the way in which features (called **characteristics**) are carried forward from parents to the next generation (called **offspring**).

4. Growth

- All organisms are made up from individual building blocks called **cells**.

- Growth is how an organism becomes bigger and sometimes more complicated.

- This is achieved by using the raw materials obtained through **nutrition**, to increase the **size** and/or **number** of cells.

✓ **Remember**: there are seven life processes but you only need to know four for the 11+ examination – nutrition, movement, reproduction and growth.

The organs in animals and plants which carry out the life processes

An **organ** is a structure which performs a particular function.

Organs in plants

- **Flower**: its main function is to **make seeds** and so the flower will contain the reproductive organs. Each seed will, with successful germination, grow into a new plant. Some flowers rely upon being visited by insects to help with reproduction. In order to attract insects, the flower will either put on an attractive display (**colour and shape of petals**), or produce a distinctive smell (**scent**), or both.

- **Leaves**: each leaf is a miniature factory, making the food which the plant needs in order for it to grow. The large, flat surfaces together with the green colour (**chlorophyll**), trap the light needed for the plant to make food by the process called **photosynthesis**.

ⓘ **Photosynthesis** is the name given to the method plants use to feed themselves – **photo** (= light); **synthesis** (= making).

- **Stem**: this does **two** important jobs: (i) **support**; (ii) **transport**.

  (i) Support:
  - Flowers need to be displayed to attract insects for reproduction.
  - Leaves need to be held up to the light.

  (ii) Transport:
  The stem contains various tubes which:
  - Move water and minerals from the roots to all parts of the plant.
  - Move food produced in the leaves to the growing and storage places.

- **Roots**: the root system has **two** main jobs to do:

  (i) To hold the plant firmly in the soil.

  (ii) To absorb water and minerals from the soil.

Organs in animals

- **Brain**: this receives messages from all parts of the body through the **nervous system** (a network of nerves connected to the brain by the spinal cord). The information in these messages is received and instructions are sent to control the life processes of movement, nutrition, reproduction and growth.

- **Lungs**: they take oxygen from the air and pass it into our blood and at the same time remove waste carbon dioxide from our blood and pass it into the air.

- **Heart**: this pumps the blood which carries digested food, oxygen and waste products to and from all parts of the body. The flow of blood needs to happen continuously to maintain life and the heart is the pump that makes this happen.

- **Stomach**: here food is mixed with chemicals as part of the digestive process.

- **Intestines**: a long tube where digested food is absorbed into the bloodstream.

- **Liver**: many chemical reactions take place here and digested food from the intestine is treated and sent to the part of the body where it is needed.

- **Kidneys**: soluble waste is filtered out here and removed from the body in the form of urine.

Adaptation – the features of organisms which fit them to their surroundings and increase their chances of survival

Domestic pets and farm animals are provided with food and shelter. This is not so for animals that live in the wild and they will have features, for example sharp claws and good eyesight, that will enable them to survive. Plants will also develop in different ways to be able to grow in different conditions.

Sample questions

Try these sample questions for yourself. The answers are given at the back of the book.

1.1   A motor car moves and uses fuel. Give **two** reasons why it cannot be said to be a
        living organism.   (2)

1.2   Give an example of a movement in plants.   (1)

1.3   Why is reproduction an important life process of organisms?   (1)

1.4   What increases when growth of an organism takes place and how is this achieved?   (2)

1.5   For the diagram below, match each of the following organs to its numbered label:

        flower   stem   root   leaf   (4)

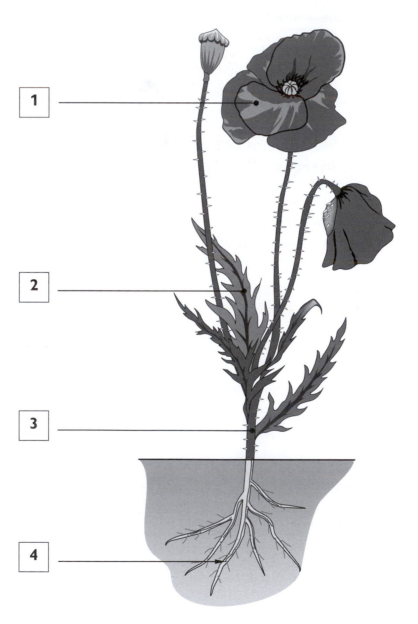

1.6   For the diagram below, match each of the following organs to its numbered label:

stomach   kidneys   liver   intestines   brain   heart   lungs   (7)

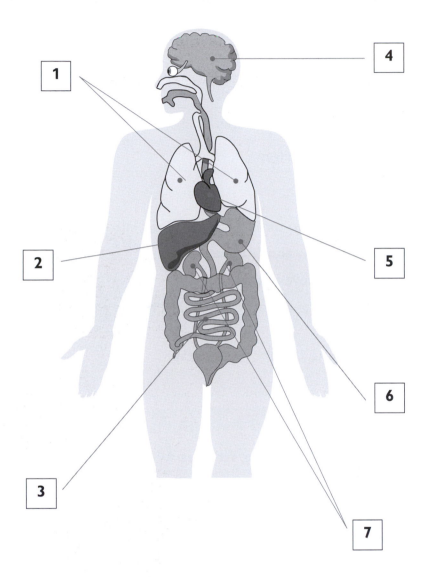

1.7   What does the word **adaptation** mean? Give an example.   (2)

1.2 Humans and other animals

Nutrition

Food is taken into the mouth where it is cut up by teeth.

Type of tooth	Shape	Function
Canine	Pointed	Tear food – killing
Incisor	Sharp-edged chisel	Cut food
Pre-molar	Two pointed ridges	Tear and grind food
Molar	Broad ridges	Grind and crush food

Care of teeth:

- A layer of bacteria called **plaque** turns sugar from food into acid.
- Acid attacks the enamel causing **tooth decay**.
- Regular brushing helps to remove plaque.
- Fluoride in water or toothpaste makes tooth enamel harder and more resistant to acid attack.
- Less sugar in the diet helps to prevent tooth decay.

Healthy eating

An intake of food provides:

- A supply of energy: required for all living activities.
- Materials which enable an organism to (i) grow, (ii) replace worn or damaged parts.

Type of food	Where found	How it is used
Carbohydrates (i) starches (ii) sugars	 Bread, pasta, rice Cakes, sweets, fruit	 Supply of energy Supply of energy
Fats	Meat, milk, butter, cheese	Store of energy, insulation
Proteins	Fish, meat, milk, eggs	Manufacture, growth and repair of cells
Mineral salts	Meat, vegetables	Calcium – bones; iron – blood

Type of food	Where found	How it is used
Vitamins	Fruit, vegetables, dairy products	To make certain chemical reactions happen that keep the body free from disease
Fibre	Cereals, fruit, vegetables	To help passage of food through the digestive system
Water	Drinks, some foods (salads)	To dissolve and transport materials

Balanced diet

A balanced diet includes a mixture of foods to provide us with all the different types of nutrients we need, in the correct proportions.

How to test for presence of starch

(i) Crush solid foods into small pieces.

(ii) Add a few drops of iodine solution.

(iii) A colour change from brown to blue-black shows that starch is present.

Circulation

- Oxygen enters the body through the lungs and into the blood.
- The heart pumps blood to all cells in **arteries**.
- Oxygen and food is carried to all cells in the blood.
- Carbon dioxide and waste materials return to the heart in **veins**.
- Blood is pumped to the lungs where carbon dioxide leaves the body.

The heart pumps blood through a contraction of the heart muscle (known as a **heartbeat** or **pulse**). Normal pulse rate is about 70 beats per minute.

Exercise means that more food and oxygen is needed by the cells so the heart beats faster to achieve this.

Benefits of exercise:
- Heart muscle is in better shape because of regular use, reducing risk of **heart attack**.
- Excess carbohydrate and fat is used up, reducing **obesity**.
- Body muscles are in better shape, increasing ability to exercise for longer (**stamina**).

How we move

Humans are **vertebrates** because they have an internal skeleton made of bones which:

- Support the body.
- Protect the brain (skull) and nerve cord (backbone or vertebral column).
- Allow movement (muscles will move those bones where there are joints).

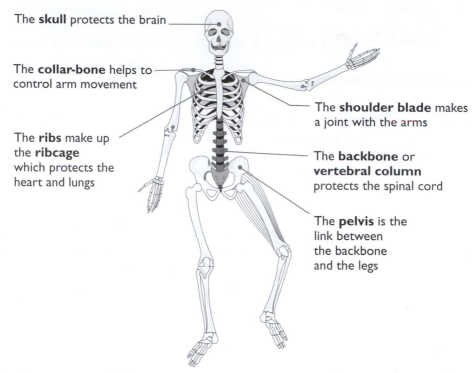

The **skull** protects the brain

The **collar-bone** helps to control arm movement

The **ribs** make up the **ribcage** which protects the heart and lungs

The **shoulder blade** makes a joint with the arms

The **backbone** or **vertebral column** protects the spinal cord

The **pelvis** is the link between the backbone and the legs

Stages in human growth and development

- **Fertilised egg**: the joining of special cells from the mother and the father.
- **Embryo**: development of the new human inside the mother.
- **Baby**: cannot feed or walk without help.
- **Child**: can feed, walk and talk but is still reliant on help from parents.
- **Puberty**: sex organs mature but growth continues.
- **Adult**: growth complete; reproduction is possible.
- **Old age**: no growth; some life processes work less well.
- **Death**: life processes come to a stop.

Healthy living

As well as having a balanced diet and taking regular exercise, it is important not to put our bodies at risk from the following:

- **Smoking tobacco**: risk of lung cancer, heart attack, difficult breathing.
- **Alcohol**: risk of damage to liver, stomach and heart.
- **Solvents and aerosols**: risk of damage to brain and suffocation.
- **Drugs**: risk of damage to many life processes and may damage the brain, liver, stomach.

Sample questions

Try these sample questions for yourself. The answers are given at the back of the book.

1.8   Make a table with the left-hand column listing the four main kinds of teeth. Fill in the right-hand column with the correct function of each type of tooth.   (8)

1.9   (a) What causes tooth decay?   (1)

     (b) List three things that you can do to prevent tooth decay.   (3)

1.10 Study the table and answer the questions below.

Food	Carbohydrate (g per 100g)	Fat (g per 100g)	Protein (g per 100g)
Orange juice	8	0	0
Bacon	0	10	12
Egg	0	5	6
Bread	24	v. small	4
Butter	0	8	v. small

     (a) Select two foods that provide a good supply of energy.   (2)

     (b) Select two foods that are good for bodybuilding and growth.   (2)

     (c) Name two important food types not included in the table.   (2)

1.11 Why will taking exercise cause the heart to move faster?   (2)

1.12 An athlete's pulse was taken three times:

        (i) just before a race;

        (ii) immediately after the race;

        (iii) 10 minutes after the race.

     How would you expect the pulse rate to change:

     (a) between tests (i) and (ii);   (1)

     (b) between tests (ii) and (iii)?   (2)

1.13 What are the three functions of a skeleton?   (3)

1.3 Green plants

(i) Growth and nutrition

All organisms require food to release energy for their life processes. Plants use sunlight as a source of energy, and carbon dioxide and water as raw materials to produce food and oxygen. Animals obtain their energy by eating plants or other animals.

ⓘ Plants are at the very start of all food chains/webs.

For healthy growth, plants need **all** of the following things (called **factors**):

- **Carbon dioxide**: taken from air for making food.

- **Oxygen**: produced in photosynthesis and needed for respiration.

- **Water**: for making food, transporting materials round the plant and maintaining structure (preventing wilting).

- **Light**: the energy supply to produce food from carbon dioxide and water (photosynthesis).

- **Warmth**: a good temperature to make chemical reactions take place in the plant.

- **Minerals**: the chemicals needed to combine with the food made by the plant, to make the various structures, such as healthy leaves, roots, flowers, fruits, e.g. **nitrates** are needed for healthy growth and **magnesium** is needed to make chloraphyll.

⚗ **Finding out how factors affect the growth of the plant**

Change **one** factor – leave the other four the same.

Measure plant growth – height/length or mass.

Where the food is made

- The green in the stem and leaves is the pigment **chlorophyll**.

- Chlorophyll traps the light energy needed for **photosynthesis**.

- Extra oxygen that is not required by the plant for its life processes is released from the leaves into the air.

- Extra food that is not required by the plant for its life processes is sent through the stem to either the growing or storage points.

How the plant obtains its minerals

- From the surrounding soil through its **roots**.

(Soils that do not have enough minerals can have them added as **fertilisers**.)

(ii) Reproduction

The variety of plants depends upon the process of **sexual reproduction** which is the fusion of male and female sex cells that are made in the sex organs. The process of carrying male pollen to a female stigma is called **pollination**. The fusion of a male pollen with a female ovule is called **fertilisation**.

1. Male sex organ: **stamen (anther + filament)**.
   Female sex organ: **carpel (stigma + style + ovary)**.

2. Male sex cells: **pollen** – are made in the **anther**.
   Female sex cells: **ovules** – are made in the **ovary**.

3. **Pollination**: the transfer of pollen from anther to stigma by various ways:

   (i) Anther and stigma in same flower (self-pollination); anther and stigma in different flowers (cross-pollination).

   (ii) Pollen carried from anther to stigma by (a) **insect** or (b) **wind**.

4. **Fertilisation**: the fusing of the sex cell pollen and ovule:

   ● Pollen grain grows a tube when it lands on the stigma.

   ● Pollen tube grows down through the style and enters the ovule through a small hole.

   Male sex cell travels down the pollen tube and fuses with the female sex cell in the ovule.

5. Fertilised ovule develops into a **seed**.

6. Wall of ovary changes and becomes a **fruit**. It contains and protects the seed/s.

7. Seeds are **dispersed** so that new plants do not compete with parent plant for nutrients, light, water and space. Seeds can be dispersed in various ways; for example:

   (i) Animals tempted by the fleshy fruit which contains indigestible seeds.

   (ii) Wind carries seeds with parachutes (dandelion) or wings (sycamore) away from parent plant.

8. The dormant seed awakens or **germinates** into a new plant.

ⓘ **WOW!**

> **Water**
>
> **Oxygen**
>
> **Warmth**

are needed for a seed to be able to germinate.

Germination: a seed changes into a young plant

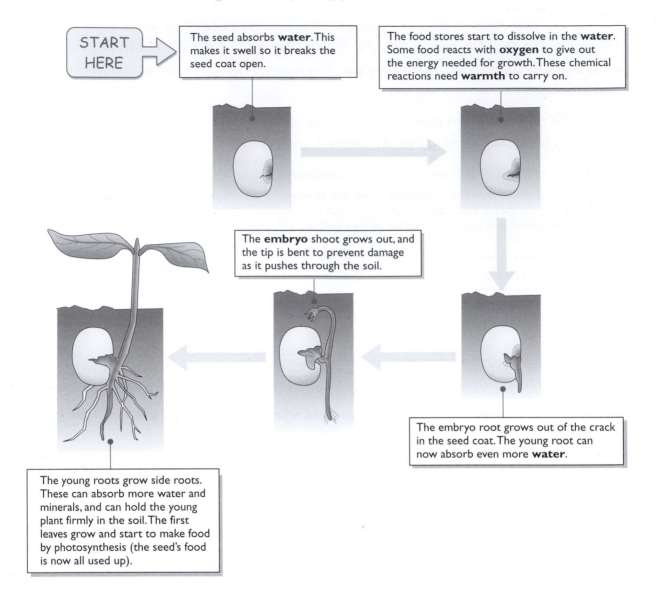

START HERE

The seed absorbs **water**. This makes it swell so it breaks the seed coat open.

The food stores start to dissolve in the **water**. Some food reacts with **oxygen** to give out the energy needed for growth. These chemical reactions need **warmth** to carry on.

The **embryo** shoot grows out, and the tip is bent to prevent damage as it pushes through the soil.

The embryo root grows out of the crack in the seed coat. The young root can now absorb even more **water**.

The young roots grow side roots. These can absorb more water and minerals, and can hold the young plant firmly in the soil. The first leaves grow and start to make food by photosynthesis (the seed's food is now all used up).

Sample questions

Try these sample questions for yourself. The answers are given at the back of the book.

1.14 Suggest why the following two gases are important to plants:
   (a) Oxygen. (1)
   (b) Carbon dioxide. (1)

1.15 Complete the table to show why the following factors are important in healthy plant growth. (5)

Factor	Why the factor is important to healthy plant growth
Air	
Light	
Warmth	
Water	
Minerals	

1.16 Select the best word from the following list to fill each of the spaces in the sentences below.

| anthers | fertilisation | ovules | apples | fruits | pollination | buds |
| germinate | stigmas | change | grow | testes | | |

(a) In flowering plants, pollen is produced by the . . . . (1)

(b) The ovaries of flowering plants contain . . . . (1)

(c) The transfer of pollen between plants is called . . . . (1)

(d) After . . . . , seeds are formed in the ovaries. (1)

(e) The ovaries, containing seeds, will develop into . . . . (1)

(f) After they have dispersed, seeds may . . . . to form seedlings. (1)

(g) Seedlings . . . . into adult plants. (1)

1.17 (a) Some flowers are pollinated by insects. Name one feature which will help to attract insects. (1)

(b) Draw a labelled diagram to show a pollen grain fertilising an ovule. (3)

1.18 In order to find out what conditions are needed for germination, some radish seeds were placed on cotton wool in four small dishes. The dishes were placed in different conditions as shown below in the table.

Dish	Condition	Result
1	On moist cotton wool in a refrigerator	No germination
2	On moist cotton wool in a dark cupboard	Seeds germinated
3	On dry cotton wool in a dark cupboard	No germination
4	On moist cotton wool on a window sill	Seeds germinated

(a) Which two dishes tell you that water is needed for germination? (2)

(b) Is light needed for germination? How do you know? (2)

(c) Which condition is not investigated by this experiment? (1)

1.4 Variation and classification

Variation

The differences between living organisms are called **variations**. We use variation to produce **keys** so that we can put organisms into groups.

Types of key

Spider or branching key

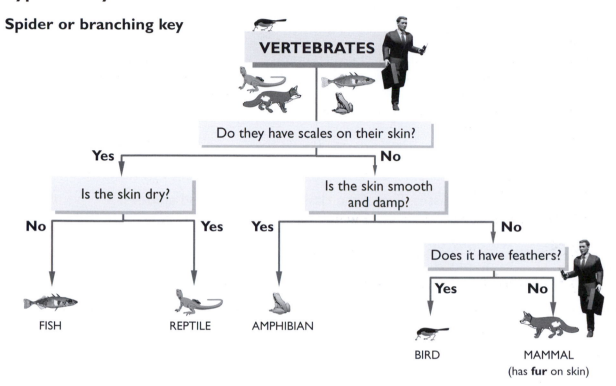

Number key

1.	Do they have scales on their skin?
	YES Go to question 2.
	NO Go to question 3.
2.	Is the skin dry?
	YES Reptile.
	NO Fish.
3.	Is the skin smooth and damp?
	YES Amphibian.
	NO Go to question 4.
4.	Does it have feathers?
	YES Bird.
	NO Mammal.

Classification

- Sorting organisms into groups is called **classification**.

- The largest groups are **kingdoms**, e.g. plant kingdom, animal kingdom.

- Kingdoms are divided into **groups**.

- Animals fall into two main groups:
  vertebrates – animals have a backbone and an internal skeleton, made of bone.
  invertebrates – animals do **not** have a backbone or a skeleton made of bone.

Arthropods – one of the sub-groups of invertebrates.

All animals in this group have:

- Jointed limbs (**arthro** = jointed; **poda** = limbs).

- Hard outer body covering.

- Segmented bodies.

The group is divided into classes. Two of the classes are **insects** and **spiders**.

Class	Number of body parts	Number of legs	Antennae	Wings	Typical example
Insect	3	6	Yes	Yes	Bee, fly, beetle
Spider	2	8	No	No	Spider, tarantula

The plant kingdom

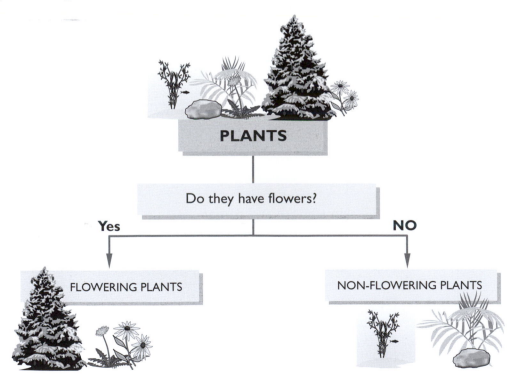

Sample questions

Try these sample questions for yourself. The answers are given at the back of the book.

1.19 Draw a spider key which displays the information about vertebrates given below:

1.	Have scales on their skin	Go to 2
	No scales	Go to 3
2.	Dry skin	reptile
	Moist skin	fish
3.	Smooth and damp skin	amphibian
	Rough and dry skin	Go to 4
4.	Has feathers	bird
	No feathers (fur on skin)	mammal

(5)

1.20 'Come into my parlour said the spider to the fly.' Explain what these two animals have (a) in common; (b) as differences between them.

(2)

1.21 Make a table with two headings, 'Invertebrate' and 'Vertebrate'. Put the subheadings **backbone**, **no backbone** and the following animals into the correct part of your table:

octopus	cat	shark	spider	frog	crab	beetle	fox

(8)

1.22 A lizard is a reptile, whilst a newt is an amphibian. In many ways they look similar, yet they belong to different classes. Give reasons for this.

(2)

1.5 Living things in their environment

ⓘ ● **Habitat**: the place where a living organism lives.

● **Environment**: **biological factors** (other plants and animals), **chemical factors** (soil, minerals, fresh/salt water) and **physical factors** (water, wind, light, temperature) affecting an organism.

Man-made changes to the environment

● Loss of agricultural land (buildings, industry, mining, transport).

● Large-scale reduction of tropical rainforests.

● Reduction of fish stocks (more efficient catching, and pollution of waters; limiting growth of fish population).

● Pollution of the air due to burning of fossil fuels, e.g. acid rain.

Conservation – man-made ways of helping the environment

● National parks, wildlife centres, zoos.

● Protection of 'endangered species'.

● More efficient engines to reduce harmful emissions when burning fossil fuels.

● Greater awareness of using 'alternative' forms of energy (wind, geothermal) to reduce pollution from burning of fossil fuels.

● Recycling of household waste to reduce landfill.

Adaptation – features of organisms that allow them to survive in their environment

● **Protection**: hard shells, prickles, ability to move quickly away from predators, camouflage (able to hide by blending in with surroundings).

● **Hunting and feeding**: sharp teeth, beaks, claws, big eyes, able to move quickly.

● **Light and length of day**:

– Spring: days become longer, triggering animal breeding, plant growth and seed germination.

– Autumn: days become shorter triggering some animals to **migrate** to warmer places and others to **hibernate** ('sleep' during the winter).

Some animals are active at night (e.g. badger, bat and hedgehog) and rest during the day. They are said to be **nocturnal**.

● **Temperature**: fur, fatty layers of insulation in polar regions.

● **Seasonal change**:

– Warming spring: increase in plant growth, return from migration; reproduction and growth during coming summer.

– Cooling autumn: leaf fall from deciduous plants; preparation for migration/hibernation.

Feeding relationships (food chains)

ⓘ A → B means A *is eaten by* B

For example:

rose leaves → aphid → ladybird → robin

rose leaves	aphid	ladybird	robin
producer	**consumer**	**consumer**	**consumer**
always a plant	a herbivore	a carnivore	top carnivore in this chain

- Plants use sunlight energy to make food so are called **producers**.

- Organisms that eat other organisms are called **consumers**.

- Animals that eat only plants are called **herbivores**.

- Animals (**predators**) that eat other animals (**prey**) are called **carnivores**.

- Animals that eat plants and animals are called **omnivores**.

Sample questions

Try these sample questions for yourself. The answers are given at the back of the book.

1.23 List three ways in which man's activities have made changes to our natural environment. (3)

1.24 List three ways in which conservation of the environment can be carried out. (3)

1.25 (a) Name two fossil fuels. (2)

   (b) Explain why the use of fossil fuels is causing problems for wildlife. (2)

1.26 Four food chains are given below:

   (i)   lettuce → rabbit → fox → flea

   (ii) oak tree → aphid → ladybird → robin

   (iii) grass → earthworm → shrew → owl

   (iv) algae → pond snail → leech → dragonfly nymph

   (a) Which food chain occurs in water? (1)

   (b) Which food chain does not contain a vertebrate? (1)

   (c) In which food chain is the herbivore a mammal? (1)

   (d) Which food chain does not contain an insect? (1)

   (e) In which food chain is the producer very much larger than the herbivore? (1)

Summary

You should now know the following:

1. The main four life processes.

2. The organs in animals and plants that carry out the life processes.

3. How organisms adapt to their surroundings.

4. Nutrition in humans and other animals.

5. The main elements of healthy eating, a balanced diet and healthy living.

6. Circulation in the body.

7. The different stages of human growth and development.

8. The growth and nutrition of green plants.

9. How green plants reproduce.

10. The main differences between living organisms and how these are classified.

11. How living organisms adapt to changing environments.

Use the glossary at the back of the book for definitions of key words.

Test yourself

Before moving on to the next chapter, make sure you can answer the following questions. The answers are at the back of the book.

1. What is an organism?

2. The four life processes in this chapter begin with the letters N, M, R and G.

   (a) Write out the full names.

   (b) These names are answers in a crossword. Write a clue so that each name can be identified correctly.

3. What do the following do: (a) heart; (b) arteries; (c) veins?

4. Name two features that are common to all arthropods.

5. Explain the following terms: (a) habitat; (b) environment.

Chapter 2: 13+ Biology

2.1 Cells and cell functions

Cells – the building blocks of life

All living organisms are made from **cells**. There is a great variety of these, as they are often constructed differently to enable them to carry out specific tasks. However, they all have features that are common to all living organisms, namely:

- **Nucleus**: the control centre of the cell. One of the main functions is the part it plays in **reproduction**. This is because all the information needed for a cell to replicate itself is carried in **genes** in the long strands of **DNA** called **chromosomes**.

- **Cytoplasm**: all living material **other than** the nucleus contains organelles which are tiny structures and each one does a particular job (for example, in mitochondria, the organnelles are where the chemical processes of respiration take place). Many of the chemical reactions, including **respiration**, take place here.

- **Cell surface membrane**: this allows the passage of certain chemicals both in and out of the cell, as well as enclosing its contents.

Plant cells

As well as containing the structures listed above, plant cells may **also contain**:

- **Cell wall**: a rigid layer made of **cellulose** that supports the cell, adds strength to the plant and lets water and gases in and out.

- **Central vacuole**: a permanent cavity filled with **sap** which is a watery fluid that helps to maintain the shape of the cell. Lack of water causes the vacuole to shrink and so rigidity of the cell is not maintained and the plant may droop (**wilt**).

- **Chloroplasts**: found in some plant cells and contain the **chlorophyll** needed for the nutritional process of **photosynthesis** to take place.

Animal and plant cells: similarities and differences

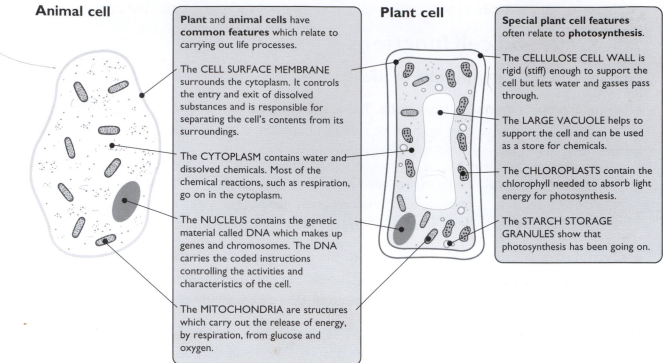

Animal cell

Plant cell

Plant and animal cells have common features which relate to carrying out life processes.

The CELL SURFACE MEMBRANE surrounds the cytoplasm. It controls the entry and exit of dissolved substances and is responsible for separating the cell's contents from its surroundings.

The CYTOPLASM contains water and dissolved chemicals. Most of the chemical reactions, such as respiration, go on in the cytoplasm.

The NUCLEUS contains the genetic material called DNA which makes up genes and chromosomes. The DNA carries the coded instructions controlling the activities and characteristics of the cell.

The MITOCHONDRIA are structures which carry out the release of energy, by respiration, from glucose and oxygen.

Special plant cell features often relate to photosynthesis.

The CELLULOSE CELL WALL is rigid (stiff) enough to support the cell but lets water and gasses pass through.

The LARGE VACUOLE helps to support the cell and can be used as a store for chemicals.

The CHLOROPLASTS contain the chlorophyll needed to absorb light energy for photosynthesis.

The STARCH STORAGE GRANULES show that photosynthesis has been going on.

13+
B

Specialised cells for specific jobs

Most larger organisms are **multi-cellular**, i.e. made up from a large number of cells of different types.

Type of cell	Shape	Function
Sperm cell	Large head, contains male genes, long tail for swimming	Fertilises female egg
Egg cell (ovum)	Larger than sperm, contains female genes	To divide cells and develop embryo after fertilisation
Muscle cell	Long, contains contractible fibrils	Becomes shorter to cause movement
Nerve cell	Long and thin	Carries messages round the body
Ciliated epithelial cells	Lining layer with little hairs (cilia)	Cilia trap dust and move it out of lungs
Root hair cells	Rectangular with 'hair' extension	'Hair' extends into soil to collect water and minerals
Pollen cell	Grows a long tube from stigma to ovary	Male nucleus fuses with nucleus in an ovum located in an ovule

Tissues and organs

Specialised cells, generally of the same type, will combine together to make **tissues**, e.g. muscles or skin.

Sometimes tissues of various kinds combine to form an **organ**, which is a structure that performs a specific function.

- The **leaf** is an **organ** which is made from various types of plant tissue.

- The **eye** is an **organ** which is made from various types of animal tissue.

Each organ has a specific job to do and in more complex animals such as mammals, organs will combine into a **system**.

Separate systems do not work independently but work together to ensure the successful development and operation of the body.

Main systems in the human body

Name of system	What it does	Main organs in the system	Location of organs
Locomotion system	Supports the body and allows movement	Muscles and skeleton of bones	Throughout the body
Transport system	Takes food to all parts of body and removes waste from them	Heart and blood vessels	Throughout the body
Respiratory system	Provides oxygen and removes carbon dioxide from body	Windpipe and lungs	Thorax
Nervous system (including sensory system)	Takes messages to/from all parts of the body via the brain	Brain, spinal cord, nerves, eyes, ears, nose, tongue	Brain – head; spinal cord – backbone; nerves – throughout the body
Digestive system	Breaks down food and absorbs useful chemicals into the blood	Gut, stomach, intestine, liver	Mouth – head; otherwise, mainly in the abdomen
Reproductive system	Produces/receives gametes for next generation	Testes, ovaries, uterus	Abdomen
Excretory system	Removes waste products	Kidneys, bladder, liver	Abdomen

Sample questions

Try these sample questions for yourself. The answers are given at the back of the book.

2.1 Do all plant cells contain chloroplasts? Give a reason for your answer. (2)

2.2 (a) Draw a sperm cell and an egg cell. (2)

  (b) Explain the differences in the shape of these cells. (2)

  (c) What is the function of these cells? (2)

2.3 This question is about the human body. Draw the table below and complete it. (14)

Name of system	What it does	Main organs in the system
Locomotion		
Transport		
Respiratory		
Nervous		
Digestive		
Reproductive		
Excretory		

2.2 Nutrition

An intake of food provides:

- A supply of energy: required for all living activities.

- Materials that enable an organism to (i) grow (ii) replace worn or damaged parts.

In general, food taken in by organisms consists of two parts:

(i) Useful materials.

(ii) Waste.

Food is broken down by **digestion**.

- Useful materials are absorbed into the cells.

- Waste materials are collected together as **faeces** and removed from the body by **egestion**.

(i) Useful materials

Protein:

- Made from long strands of amino acids folded over into special shapes.

- Used for growth and repair of cells. Manufacture of **enzymes** used to control chemical reactions.

- Found in meats, fish, milk, cheese, eggs, nuts, green vegetables and flour.

Carbohydrates:

- Compounds containing the elements carbon, hydrogen and oxygen.

- Two main groups:
  (i) sugars, e.g. glucose – these may be found in fruits, jams, soft drinks and sweets.
  (ii) starches (built up from sugars and stored in the muscles and liver until needed to be broken down into glucose for respiration) – these may be found in potatoes, nuts, rice, cereals, peas, beans, bread and cakes.

> ⚗ **How to test for presence of starch**
>
> (i) Crush solid foods into small pieces.
>
> (ii) Add a few drops of iodine solution.
>
> (iii) A colour change from brown to blue-black shows that starch is present.

Fats:

- Used as a store of energy (can be broken down into glucose for respiration) and also as a layer of insulation.

- Found in meats, dairy products and food fried in animal fats, e.g. chips.

Vitamins and minerals:

- These are needed in **small amounts** to enable important chemical reactions to happen.

- They are not produced by the body, so have to be taken in with food.

Name	What it is needed for	Where found	Result of lack of it
Vitamin C	Tissue repair, resistance to disease	Fresh fruit and vegetables	Scurvy (bleeding gums), poor growth in children, tissue repair is very slow
Calcium	Making of bones, teeth and blood clotting	Dairy products, flour products, green vegetables	Poor bone development
Iron	Manufacture of red blood cells	Meat, green vegetables	Shortages of red blood cells

Water:

- Present in every living cell and forms about 70% of our bodies.

- The blood system moves materials that have been dissolved in water.

- Egg and sperm cells move around our bodies in fluids which are mainly water.

- Humans lose about 1.5 litres of water each day in urine, sweat and breath.

- Water can be replaced (i) as a drink, (ii) in foods such as salads.

Fibre:

- Comes from plants and is mainly indigestible.

- Provides bulk to enable food to travel through the digestive system more efficiently.

- Found in cereals, whole grain bread and vegetables.

(ii) Balanced diet

All of the groups of nutrients listed above are needed.

- An all-meat diet provides a good source of protein, but also too much fat and almost no carbohydrate.

- An all-potato diet provides plenty of carbohydrate, but very little protein.

We need to have a mixture of foods to provide us with these in the right proportions. This is called a **balanced diet**.

(iii) Digestion

Much of the food that we eat will consist of a mixture of proteins, fats and carbohydrates which need to be broken down into smaller soluble molecules. Much of this breaking down will be carried out by **enzymes**. An important enzyme is **amylase** which breaks starch into simple sugars.

Enzymes:

- These are chemicals which enable other chemical reactions to happen.

- There is a different enzyme for each chemical reaction in the body.

- Enzymes do not change as they work, so can be used again.

Stages of digestion:

Ingestion: food is taken into the mouth.
Physical digestion: teeth cut and break down food which is mixed with saliva produced in the mouth.
Chemical digestion: action of enzymes break down food into small, soluble molecules which can be dissolved in the blood.
Absorption: soluble food molecules move across the villi, which are part of the walls of the small intestine, into the bloodstream which carries them to the liver for sorting, then to all parts of the body.
Assimilation: digested food is used by the cells for growth and repair.
Egestion: in the large intestine, undigested food mixed with fibre becomes faeces and passes out through the anus.

Sample questions

Try these sample questions for yourself. The answers are given at the back of the book.

2.4 Below is a table showing relative amounts of different nutrients in food that might be eaten at breakfast.

Food	Carbohydrate (g per 100g)	Fat (g per 100g)	Protein (g per 100g)
Orange juice	8	0	0
Bacon	0	10	12
Egg	0	5	6
Bread	24	v. small	4
Butter	0	8	v. small

(a) Select a food which is a good supply of energy. (1)

(b) Select two foods which are good for bodybuilding and growth. (2)

(c) What is the main carbohydrate found in (i) orange juice; (ii) bread? (2)

(d) Name two important nutrients not included in the table. (2)

2.5 The following table shows the average daily amounts of protein which human males, of different ages, require if they are to remain fit and healthy.

Age (in years)	11	14	18	25	45	65
Protein requirement (in g/day)	75	85	100	65	65	65

Explain the differences in protein requirement for human males at ages 18 and 45. (4)

2.6

	Snack X	Snack Y
Fat	22%	34%
Fibre	18%	35%
Sugar	60%	31%

(a) (i) Which snack contains the greatest amount of fibre? (1)

(ii) Suggest why fibre is an important part of your diet. (1)

(b) (i) Which snack would you eat before running a race? (1)

(ii) Give a reason for your answer. (1)

2.7 Vitamins and minerals are important parts of our diets. Give one example of each, suggesting what they do. (4)

2.3 Movement in humans

The skeleton

- The skeleton has three main functions:

   (i) To **support** the tissues and organs.

   (ii) To **protect** delicate organs, e.g. backbone – spinal cord; skull – brain; ribcage – heart and lungs.

   (iii) To enable **movement** to take place.

- There are just over 200 bones in the human body.

- Bones are made of cells located within layers of calcium phosphate (a hard material).

- In the centre of the bone is the bone marrow where new bone cells (and red blood cells) are formed.

- Leg bones, which have to support the whole body, are much larger than the arm bones.

- Arms and legs move because the bones are levers which pivot about joints (**synovial joints**).

- Bones are joined together by ligaments.

A synovial joint

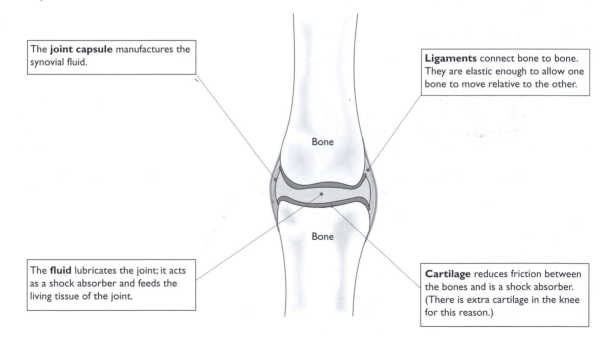

The **joint capsule** manufactures the synovial fluid.

Ligaments connect bone to bone. They are elastic enough to allow one bone to move relative to the other.

Bone

Bone

The **fluid** lubricates the joint; it acts as a shock absorber and feeds the living tissue of the joint.

Cartilage reduces friction between the bones and is a shock absorber. (There is extra cartilage in the knee for this reason.)

How are bones able to move?

● This is achieved by the action of opposing (**antagonistic**) pairs of muscles.

● Muscles are attached to bones by non-elastic threads called **tendons**.

● Muscles are made of long cells grouped together to form fibres that are packed together in a sheath.

● Muscle fibres shorten (**contract**) when a signal is received from the nervous system.

● When muscle action is no longer required, the muscle **relaxes** and goes back to its original length.

ⓘ **Muscles can only contract – they never push.**

A. Action of the biceps muscle bending

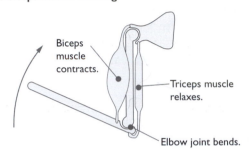

Biceps muscle contracts.

Triceps muscle relaxes.

Elbow joint bends.

B. Action of the triceps muscle

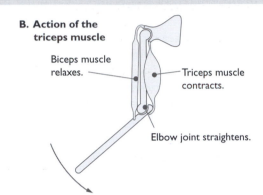

Biceps muscle relaxes.

Triceps muscle contracts.

Elbow joint straightens.

Sample questions

Try these sample questions for yourself. The answers are given at the back of the book.

2.8   What are the functions of a skeleton? (3)

2.9   (a) Why are muscles that are used for controlled movement at a joint found in pairs? (2)

   (b) Give an example of one pair. (1)

   (c) What is the general name given to the type of paired muscles in (b)? (1)

2.10   What is the function of the following skeletal structures?

   (a) Skull. (1)

   (b) Vertebrae (backbone). (1)

   (c) Ribs. (1)

2.11   (a) What is the hard mineral found in bone? (1)

   (b) What is bone marrow? (State where it can be found and what it does.) (2)

2.4 Reproduction in humans

- **Sexual reproduction** requires two individuals (**parents**), male and female.

- During **puberty**, humans develop reproductive organs which produce the sex cells – **sperm** (**male**) and **ova** (**female**) – called **gametes**.

- The gametes are brought together (during copulation) and fuse to form a fertilised egg (**zygote**).

- The zygote will, after much cell division, grow into an embryo which then develops into a new individual.

13+

B

Puberty – a time of physical change

- Occurs between the ages of 10 and 20.

- Body hair starts growing, e.g. hair around the genitals (pubic hair).

- In males, hair grows on chest and face and voice becomes deeper.

- In females, the menstrual cycle begins.

- Reproductive organs develop, e.g. in males, penis becomes larger; in females, breasts develop and hips become wider.

Adolescence – a time of emotional change

- Occurs after puberty.

- Boys and girls become more independent and more responsible for their thoughts and actions.

- Boys and girls become more aware of the opposite sex.

- As there is great variation in the time when the changes begin and also in the nature and size of these, some people may become anxious because they appear to develop earlier or later than their friends.

The menstrual cycle

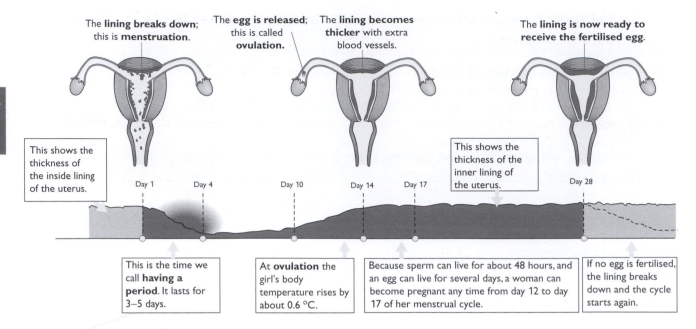

The **lining breaks down;** this is **menstruation.**

The **egg is released;** this is called **ovulation.**

The **lining becomes thicker** with extra blood vessels.

The **lining is now ready to receive the fertilised egg.**

This shows the thickness of the inside lining of the uterus.

This shows the thickness of the inner lining of the uterus.

Day 1   Day 4   Day 10   Day 14   Day 17   Day 28

This is the time we call **having a period**. It lasts for 3–5 days.

At **ovulation** the girl's body temperature rises by about 0.6 °C.

Because sperm can live for about 48 hours, and an egg can live for several days, a woman can become pregnant any time from day 12 to day 17 of her menstrual cycle.

If no egg is fertilised, the lining breaks down and the cycle starts again.

Fertilisation and implantation

- During sexual intercourse, special sponge tissue (**erectile tissue**) within the penis becomes full of blood which enables the penis to become stiff enough to enter the female's vagina.

- Movement of the penis within the vagina causes a **nervous reflex** which is a signal for over 300 million sperms contained in about 4–5 cm³ of fluid to be **ejaculated** out of the penis into the vagina.

- **One** egg is released by the female every 28 days and is carried by cilia into the **oviduct**.

- Only a small proportion of sperms will complete the journey to the oviduct and it is here that **only one** sperm will fuse with the egg to form a **zygote**.

- The zygote contains **genes** from both the mother and father.

- The zygote begins cell division until a ball of about 128 cells (now called an embryo) arrives in the uterus and settles deep in the newly-formed thick lining.

- This settling process is called **implantation**.

- Once the embryo is implanted, the mother is said to be **pregnant**.

Development of the embryo

- The implanted embryo develops into the **fetus** by means of cell division and specialisation.

- The fetus is contained within a sac (**amniotic sac** filled with **amniotic fluid**) and is attached to the **placenta** by the **umbilical cord**.

The placenta

- The placenta is a plate-shaped organ that grows deep into the uterus wall and increases in size as the fetus develops.

- It enables food and oxygen to be passed to the fetus and carbon dioxide together with waste materials to be removed from the fetus.

- Although the mother's blood system flows close to the blood vessels of the fetus, the two are **entirely different** systems.

(i) The blood of the mother and the blood of the fetus do not mix. This is because:

- The blood group of the fetus may be different from that of the mother. Bloods of different groups must **not** be mixed together.

- The mother's blood pressure will be **much higher** than that of the fetus.

The umbilical cord

- Contains blood vessels that:
  - Take oxygen and food **to** the fetus.
  - Take carbon dioxide and nitrogenous waste **away from** the fetus.

- It is clamped at birth to prevent bleeding and then cut. The 'belly button' is the remains of the umbilical cord.

Care during pregnancy

Pregnant mothers should be careful about their lifestyle and diet. This is because:

- Smoking and alcohol intake by the mother, together with germs from diseases, could result in harmful materials being passed to the fetus through the umbilical cord.

- Excess physical activity may harm the fetus.

Birth

- After a gestation period of about 40 weeks (9 months), **labour** begins with contractions of the uterus.

- Contractions cause the amniotic sac to burst and fluid flows out of the vagina; this is called the **breaking of the waters**.

- Further contractions push the baby, head first, out into the world.

- Once the newborn baby is breathing, the umbilical cord is clamped and then cut.

Sample questions

Try these sample questions for yourself. The answers are given at the back of the book.

2.12 (a) Where does fertilisation usually take place? (1)

   (b) (i) What happens to the wall of the uterus if fertilisation does not take place? (1)

   (ii) What is this process called? (1)

   (iii) What is the name of the cycle of which the process in (ii) is a part? (1)

   (iv) What is the average duration of the cycle named in (iii)? (1)

2.13 The fetus is attached to the wall of the uterus by the placenta and umbilical cord.

   (a) Name one substance that passes across the placenta from the fetus to the mother. (1)

   (b) Name two substances that pass across the placenta from the mother to the fetus. (2)

2.14 Explain why the blood system of the mother is an entirely different system from the blood system of the fetus. (2)

2.15 State two ways in which the fetus will be protected whilst it is developing in the uterus. (2)

2.5 Respiration and breathing in humans

Respiration

> (i) Important note: respiration is **not** breathing.

- Respiration is a series of **chemical reactions** carried out within each living cell to release energy for all life processes.

- Respiration can be summarised by the following equation:

$$\boxed{\text{glucose + oxygen}} \rightarrow \boxed{\text{carbon dioxide + water + energy}}$$

- Glucose comes from **digested foods**.

- Oxygen comes from the **air** inhaled into the lungs during **breathing**. So this form of respiration is called **aerobic** (aer = air) respiration.

- Glucose and oxygen are called **reactants**.

- Carbon dioxide and water are **waste products**.

- Both reactants and products are carried to and from the cells in the bloodstream (also called the **circulatory system**).

- Oxygen enters and carbon dioxide leaves the bloodstream by passing through the walls of **air sacs** which are part of the lungs. This is known as **gas exchange**.

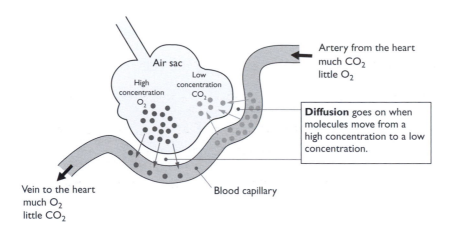

Breathing in humans

- The main organs for gas exchange are the **lungs** which are located in the thorax (chest).

- The thorax is lined with a membrane and the floor of the thorax is separated from the abdomen by a flexible membrane called the **diaphragm**.

- Muscular action by the ribs causes the diaphragm to move up and down, allowing air to move in and out of the lungs during breathing.

- Air moves in and out through the nose and throat which is connected to the windpipe (**trachea**).

- In the lungs, the trachea branches into two smaller tubes, one branch (**bronchus**) supplying each lung.

- Each bronchus divides into smaller branches (**bronchioles**), which divide again and again.

- At the end of each of the tiniest branches are little **air sacs** which are surrounded by blood vessels.

(i) It is **not** true to say we breathe in oxygen and breathe out carbon dioxide, for we breathe in **air**, most of which is nitrogen.

	Content of inhaled air	Content of exhaled air
Nitrogen	approx. 80%	approx. 80%
Oxygen	approx. 20%	approx. 16%
Carbon dioxide	approx. 0.04%	approx. 4%

Dangers of smoking tobacco

Tobacco smoke contains substances which harm the lungs, heart and circulation. The smoke is acidic and contains many chemicals which damage human tissue. Three of the most damaging are listed below:

- **Nicotine**: damages blood vessels leading to increase of blood pressure and risk of heart disease; causes addiction.

- **Tar**: causes lung cancer; blocks the action of cilia which sweep away dust and microbes.

- **Carbon monoxide**: reduces supply of oxygen to the cells; contributes to disease of the heart and arteries.

Sample questions

Try these sample questions for yourself. The answers are given at the back of the book.

2.16 (a) What does the word **respiration** describe? (2)

 (b) Where, in an organism, does respiration take place? (1)

2.17 (a) Write down the equation that represents aerobic respiration. (6)

 (b) What does the term **aerobic** mean? (1)

2.18 (a) In which part of the lungs does gas exchange take place? (1)

 (b) During this process, state what happens to (i) oxygen; (ii) carbon dioxide. (1)

2.19 It is often said that, 'We breathe in oxygen and breathe out carbon dioxide'. Explain why this statement is not completely correct. (2)

2.20 List three substances that enter the body because of smoking and say in which way each substance is harmful to the body. (6)

2.6 Being healthy

Healthy lifestyle

Humans can choose whether their **lifestyle** is healthy or not.

A healthy lifestyle depends upon three main factors:

(i) A **balanced diet**: a mix of protein, carbohydrate, fats, fibre, water, minerals and vitamins is needed for growth and repair/replacement of cells. Overeating of fatty and sugary foods can lead to being overweight (**obese**) which puts an extra strain on the heart as more energy is required to carry out life processes, e.g. movement.

(ii) Taking **regular exercise**: greater intake of air during exercise causes the muscles of the heart to beat faster and so remain healthy, resulting in less chance of heart disease. Excess fat in the body is reduced by exercise.

(iii) **Avoiding intake of harmful substances**:

- **Smoking** leads to lung, circulatory system and heart problems.

- **Alcohol** slows reactions and excess amounts cause damage to the liver, stomach and heart.

- **Drugs** (other than those prescribed for medical reasons) introduce chemicals into our bodies that upset the finely balanced chemical mechanism which exists to keep all our life functions working properly. Solvents, aerosols, LSD, ecstasy are examples of substances that badly damage the brain and heart.

Fighting disease

ⓘ Diseases are either non-infectious (not caught from somebody else) or infectious (caught from somebody else).

Causes of infectious diseases

Minute microorganisms (**microbes**) divide and reproduce very rapidly and can damage cells or release **toxins** (poisons) that can make you feel very ill.

- **Viruses**:

  - Must invade a living cell to reproduce, eventually causing damage to the cell.

  - When they are in a **host** cell, viruses cannot be destroyed without damaging the cell.

  - Viruses cannot be controlled by antibiotics.

  - Examples of diseases caused by viruses include influenza ('flu), common cold, AIDS.

- **Bacteria**:

  - Live and grow outside living cells.

  - Can reproduce every 20 minutes.

  - Are bigger than viruses, but smaller than cells.

  - Can be killed by **antibiotics** – taken as medicine; **antiseptics** – on the skin; **disinfectants** – on kitchen and bathroom surfaces.

  - Examples of diseases caused by bacteria include cholera, tetanus, food poisoning.

Natural defences

ⓘ Our body has three natural defences against disease: barriers, white blood cells and blood clots.

- Skin, wax in ears, tears in eyes all form barriers to keep microbes away from the body's tissues.

- White blood cells: there are two main types:
  - (i) **Phagocytes** engulf and digest microbes.
  - (ii) **Lymphocytes** recognise and produce special proteins called **antibodies** which make the microbe inactive before being destroyed by a phagocyte.

- Open wounds are protected from microbes by blood clots that are produced by a special type of blood cell (**platelet**) forming a scab.

Human actions

- **Personal hygiene**:

  - Regular washing of hands, hair and the body removes bacteria which cause body odours, infestations in hair and spread of food poisoning.

  - Regular brushing of teeth removes bacteria that cause tooth decay.

- **Community actions**:

  - Provision of safe, clean drinking water.

  - Removal and safe disposal of refuse and sewage.

  - Provision of medical care.

- **Provision of medical care**:

  - Immunisation.

  - Medicines such as antibiotics.

13+

B

2.7 Green plants as organisms

Photosynthesis – making food

(photo = light; synthesis = making)

- Photosynthesis is the **one** process which is able to use light energy to produce chemicals that are useful to **all** living organisms.

- Light energy from the Sun is changed into chemical energy and stored within the plant, enabling it to grow larger causing an **increase in biomass.**

- **Biomass** can be used as a **fuel (wood/peat)** which releases energy when it combines with oxygen during burning. **Coal** is **fossilized biomass. Oil** and **gas** are fossilised remains of **animals** that have eaten biomass.

- **Biomass** can be used as a **food.** Animals cannot carry out photosynthesis, so they have to obtain their energy by eating plants, or eating other animals that have eaten plants.

- **Plants are at the very start of all food chains/webs** – this is why they are called **primary producers.**

Photosynthesis releases oxygen into the air

- Before the arrival of green plants on the Earth, there was **no oxygen at all** in the atmosphere.

- Photosynthesis produces more oxygen than the plant needs for respiration, so excess oxygen is released into the atmosphere through the **stomata** (little holes on the underside of leaves).

- As a result of the evolution and development of green plants, the amount of oxygen in the atmosphere has built up to its present level of about 20% of all the gases in the air. So every leaf and blade of grass helps to maintain the amount of oxygen in the air.

- Oxygen needs to be replaced because respiration by **all organisms** (including plants) **removes** vast quantities of oxygen from the air every minute. If this oxygen were not **replaced by photosynthesis**, then all the oxygen would be removed from the air in a few thousand years.

Photosynthesis recycles carbon

- The element carbon is present in **all** living organisms and fossil fuels.

Organism	Carbon content
Animals	about 20%
Plants	about 4%
Fossil fuels (coal)	about 90%

- Carbon atoms can join with each other to form chains or rings to produce the complex **organic compounds** that are found in **all living organisms**.

- **Hydrocarbons** contain **carbon** and **hydrogen** (e.g. natural gas, crude oil – a mixture of many hydrocarbons).

- **Carbohydrates** contain **carbon**, **hydrogen and oxygen** (e.g. sugars, starches).

Photosynthesis uses **carbon dioxide** and **water** to produce **carbohydrates (biomass)**.

ⓘ Photosynthesis **increases** biomass and **reduces** the amount of carbon dioxide in the air.

Respiration uses **oxygen** to change carbohydrate (**biomass**) into **carbon dioxide** and **water** with energy being released.

ⓘ Respiration **reduces** biomass and **increases** the amount of carbon dioxide in the air.

Actions of man affecting the balance of gases in the air

1. Burning fossil fuels **increases** amount of carbon dioxide in the air.

2. Cutting down forests **reduces** amount of photosynthesis, so amount of carbon dioxide in the air increases because less is being used up.

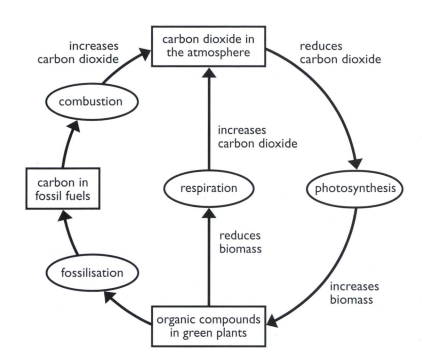

Photosynthesis – the process

1. **Part played by chloroplasts:**

    ● Energy from the Sun is absorbed within the chloroplasts which contain the green pigment **chlorophyll**, which reacts with light.

    ● Chloroplasts are found in the cytoplasm of nearly every leaf and stem cell and it is these that give plants their green colour.

    ● There are **no chloroplasts within root cells**, as photosynthesis will not happen underground where there is no light.

2. **Parts played by carbon dioxide and water:**

● These two substances provide the ingredients (carbon, hydrogen, oxygen), for the making of carbohydrates.

● Water is a supply of hydrogen: Carbon dioxide supplies carbon and oxygen.

The series of reactions that make up the process of photosynthesis may be summarised by the following word equation:

$$\text{carbon dioxide + water} \xrightarrow[\text{chlorophyll}]{\text{light energy}} \text{glucose + oxygen}$$

● Carbon dioxide and water are the **reactants** – glucose and oxygen are the **products** of photosynthesis.

What happens to the products of photosynthesis?

1. **Oxygen**

(a) Some of this will be used by the plant itself, for **respiration.**

(b) Oxygen not used by the plant will be released through the **stomata** – see above.

2. **Glucose – a carbohydrate**

(a) **Respiration**

● Photosynthesis provides the glucose which is needed by **every living cell**, for respiration.

● The leaves make more glucose than they need, so glucose is transported to other parts of the plant for respiration by a process called **translocation.**

(b) **Making living material – increasing biomass**

● For growth, plants need a constant supply of proteins and fats which can be made from sugars such as glucose.

● To make proteins, **nitrogen** will be needed as well as sugars.

● To make chlorophyll, **magnesium** will be needed as well as sugars.

(c) **Changing glucose into starch**

● In good light (daytime), glucose is made at a faster rate than the rate at which it can be transported away, so this excess glucose is changed into starch.

● In darkness (night), starch in the leaves is changed back into glucose and transported to other parts of the plant.

● Food, in the form of starch, is stored in preparation for the growth of the next generation:
 – in **seeds** (peas and beans)
 – in storage organs such as **bulbs** (onions) and **tubers** (potatoes)
 – in specialised **root systems** (carrots, parsnips)

Testing that light is needed for photosynthesis to take place and for presence of starch

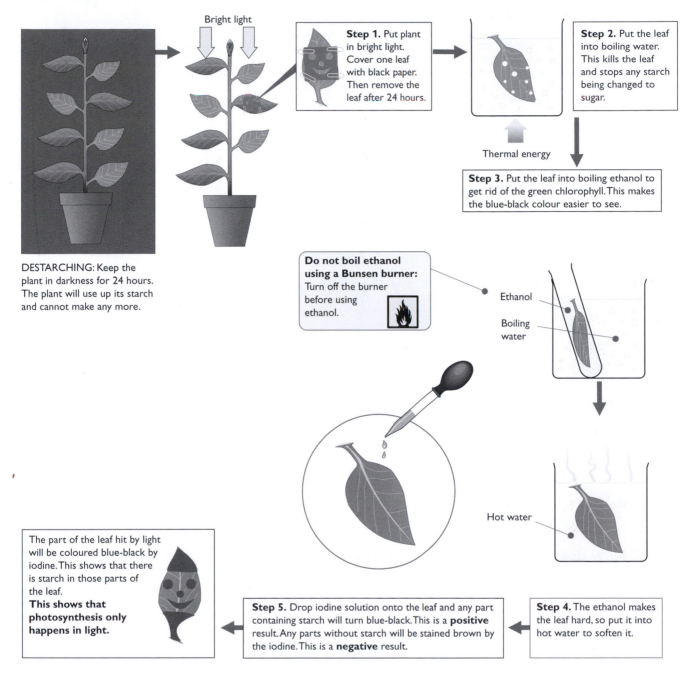

Bright light

Step 1. Put plant in bright light. Cover one leaf with black paper. Then remove the leaf after 24 hours.

Step 2. Put the leaf into boiling water. This kills the leaf and stops any starch being changed to sugar.

Thermal energy

Step 3. Put the leaf into boiling ethanol to get rid of the green chlorophyll. This makes the blue-black colour easier to see.

DESTARCHING: Keep the plant in darkness for 24 hours. The plant will use up its starch and cannot make any more.

Do not boil ethanol using a Bunsen burner: Turn off the burner before using ethanol.

Ethanol

Boiling water

Hot water

The part of the leaf hit by light will be coloured blue-black by iodine. This shows that there is starch in those parts of the leaf.
This shows that photosynthesis only happens in light.

Step 5. Drop iodine solution onto the leaf and any part containing starch will turn blue-black. This is a **positive** result. Any parts without starch will be stained brown by the iodine. This is a **negative** result.

Step 4. The ethanol makes the leaf hard, so put it into hot water to soften it.

Testing that photosynthesis produces oxygen as a waste gas

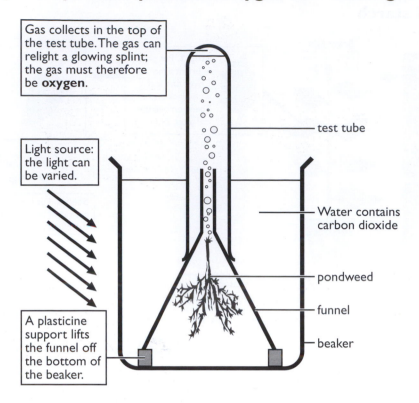

Gas collects in the top of the test tube. The gas can relight a glowing splint; the gas must therefore be **oxygen**.

Light source: the light can be varied.

A plasticine support lifts the funnel off the bottom of the beaker.

test tube

Water contains carbon dioxide

pondweed

funnel

beaker

Requirements for growth and healthy plants

1. **Water**

    ● Plants will absorb water from the surrounding soil through the root system.

    ● Water enters the root system through very thin-walled specialised cells called **root hairs**.

    How does a plant USE the water it obtains through the roots?

    (i)   As a **raw material** for **photosynthesis**.

    (ii) As a solvent for **sugars and starches**, to enable them to be moved around the plant easily.

    (iii) As a solvent for **minerals**, to enable them to be transported to the place where they will be made into the **proteins** and chemicals which are essential to the growth and development of the plant.

    (iv) To maintain physical strength of the plant by keeping the cells **turgid**. (Within each cell, the central vacuole is full of sap, which has a high water content that presses outwards making the cell rigid – or **turgid**).

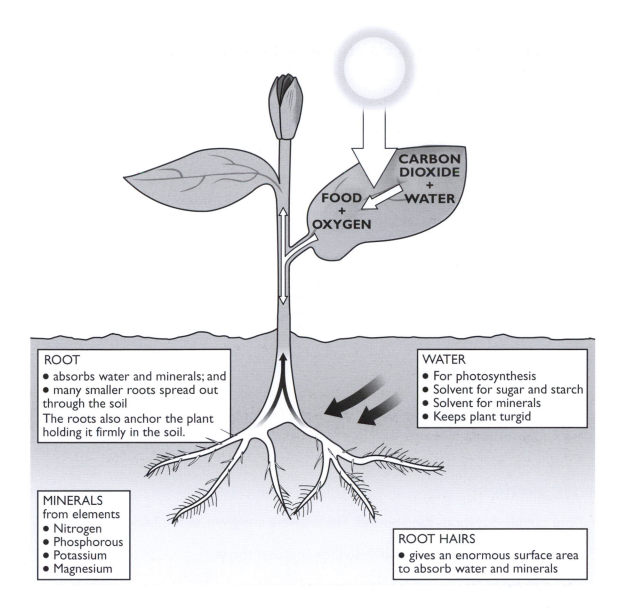

2. **Mineral salts**

- Apart from oxygen, water and carbon dioxide, a healthy plant needs supplies of the following elements:

    (i) **Nitrogen** – to make proteins that are present in all parts of the plant.

    (ii) **Phosphorous** – to help in root growth and fruit ripening.

    (iii) **Potassium** – for protection against diseases and to help with growth of seeds.

    (iv) **Magnesium** – for production of **chlorophyll** inside the chloroplasts.

- All these elements will be obtained from the soil surrounding the plant in the form of mineral salts which are soluble in water, e.g. nitrogen in the form of **nitrates**.

- Soluble mineral salts will enter the plant through the thin-walled cells called **root hair cells**.

- The large number of root hair cells **increases the surface area** of the root in contact with the soil, which enables water and soluble minerals to enter the plant more easily.

How the soluble nitrates which are found in the soil are formed

(i) **Lightning**

The intense heat in the air around a lightning strike causes nitrogen and oxygen to combine to form nitrogen oxides that dissolve in the falling rain. The soluble oxides combine with other chemicals to form nitrates.

(ii) **Action of bacteria**

There are types of bacteria (called **nitrogen fixing bacteria**) which live in nodules (lumps) in the roots of some plants (e.g. peas, beans, clover); they are able to change the nitrogen gas from the air into nitrates.

(iii) **Decay of organisms**

Dead animals and plants contain nitrogen compounds such as proteins, amino acids and urea. **Decomposers** such as fungi and bacteria act on these dead remains releasing nitrates into the soil.

(iv) **Artificial fertilisers**

Nitrates are either used up by plants or washed away by rainwater. To counteract this loss, nitrates are added to the soil in the form of soluble fertilizers such as **ammonium nitrate**.

Sample questions

Try these sample questions for yourself. The answers are given at the back of the book.

2.25 Write a word equation which describes photosynthesis. (3)

2.26 Your class has been studying photosynthesis in plants.
(a) What is the name of the pigment which reacts with light? (1)
(b) What is the colour of this pigment? (1)
(c) Where can this pigment be found? Give as much detail as you can. (1)
(d) Say, giving a reason, where in a plant you will **not** find this pigment. (1)

2.27 Your class has set up an experiment to test that starch is produced by plants.
(a) What substance do you use to test for the presence of starch? (1)
(b) Describe the colour change that takes place when starch is present. (1)
(c) Explain why you generally test for starch, rather than glucose. (1)

2.8 Variation and Classification

Variation

Although humans belong to the same species of animals (*homo sapiens*)), there are clearly differences between individuals called **variations**.

- Colour of eyes, blood group, face shape and whether you are male or female are **variations** between humans which result **only** from **genes** that are inherited from parents. These variations are called **discontinuous variations**.

- Discontinuous variations enable **easy grouping** of organisms; there are no in-between groups, e.g. one is either male or female.

- Height, shape, weight and build are variations which result **both** from **inherited genes** and the **environment**. Clearly, the amount of food intake and exercise will have an effect on all of these variations as well as those caused by the passing on of genes. These variations are called **continuous variations**.

- Continuous variations are **not easy** to put into discrete groups as there are many groups for each particular feature, e.g. size of chest.

Classification

- Sorting organisms into groups is called **classification**.

- The largest groups of organisms are known as **kingdoms**.

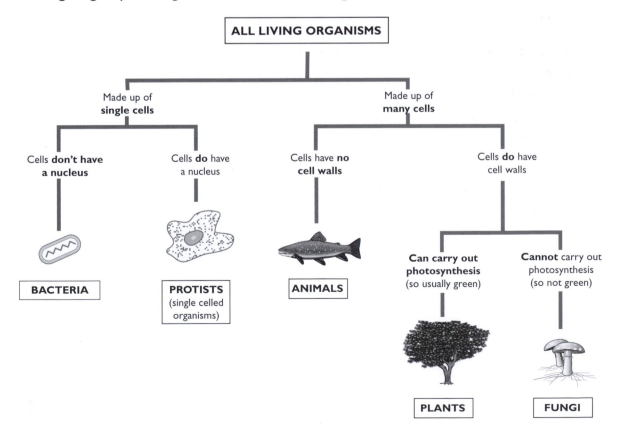

Why are fungi and green plants in different kingdoms?

- **Green plants** have chloroplasts and make their own food by photosynthesis.

- **Fungi** feed on the dead remains of other organisms. They do not have any chloroplasts.

Two main groups within the animal kingdom

1. **Invertebrates** – have no backbone. Numerous main groups called phyla (sing. phylum).

Arthropoda – an important invertebrate phylum

ALL animals in this phylum have:

- Jointed limbs in pairs (arthro = jointed; poda = limbs).

- Hard outer covering (exoskeleton) made of chitin or lime.

- Bodies divided into segments (compartments).

This is the largest of all animal groups and is divided into four main classes:

(i)   **Insects** – bee, fly, beetle

(ii) **Spiders**

(iii) **Crustaceans** – prawn, lobster, crab (woodlouse on land)

(iv) **Myriapods** – centipede, millipede.

Differences between insects and spiders

Insects	Spiders
3 body parts	2 body parts
head; thorax; abdomen	head/thorax; abdomen
6 legs (3 pairs)	8 legs (4 pairs)
antennae	no antennae
usually 2 pairs of wings	no wings

2. **Vertebrates** – have a backbone made of interlocking bones called vertebrae which protect the nerve cord which is connected to the brain that is located in the skull and is itself protected by bone.

- Vertebrates are members of a single phylum in which there are **five** main groups (**classes**) of vertebrates:

Class	Features	Examples
Fish	**all** live in water bodies covered in scales lay eggs in water cold-blooded	haddock, cod, shark
Amphibians	live on land and/or water moist smooth skin lay eggs in **water** cold-blooded	frog, toad, newt
Reptiles	scaly skin live on land and/or water lay **shelled eggs on land** cold-blooded	snake, crocodile, turtle
Birds	skin covered with feathers lay shelled eggs on land warm-blooded	eagle, blackbird, emu
Mammals	skin covered in hair or fur young born alive and fed by 　milk produced in the 　mother's mammary glands warm-blooded	dog, elephant, whale, man

- **Cold-blooded animals** – body temperature **changes** according to the temperature of the surrounding air or water.

- **Warm-blooded animals** – keep a **constant** body temperature.

The plant kingdom

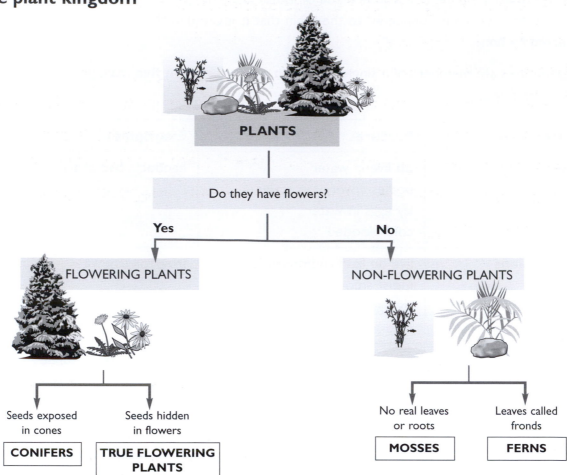

Sample questions

Try these sample questions for yourself. The answers are given at the back of the book.

2.28 Grass, rabbits and mushrooms are all organisms found in a wood, and yet they are all placed in different kingdoms. Explain why. (3)

2.29 To which type of variation do weight and athletic ability belong and from what do these result. (2)

2.30 'Come into my parlour said the spider to the fly.' Explain what these two animals
(a) have in common (2)
(b) have as differences between them. (2)

2.31 A lizard is a reptile, whilst a newt is an amphibian. They are both vertebrates and look similar in many ways. Say why biologists put them in different classes. (3)

2.9 Living things in their environment

Life, as we know it, without green plants would not exist at all.

- There would be no oxygen in the atmosphere.

- There would be no food – vegetables, salads, fruit or meat from animals that have fed on plants.

The most important resource on Earth is the **fertile soil** which is necessary to grow plants.

- Rock and sand change into fertile soil by the addition of **humus**.

- Humus is plant and animal material which has been decayed by fungi and/or bacteria.

Life depends upon the interaction of a variety of living organisms.

- The study of this interaction is known as **ecology**.

Some key words

Habitat

All organisms need a place to live which will provide them with:

    (i)   food

    (ii) shelter

    (iii) protection from predators.

The place where a living organism lives is called its **habitat**. Examples of habitats include a pond, a field, a hedgerow, a wood, your house.

Community

This refers to **all of the living organisms** within a habitat.

The community will consist of a collection of **populations**.

A population is a collection of organisms of the same species.

ⓘ A **habitat** (a place) and the **communities** (populations of living organisms), add together to make an **ecosystem**.

Ecology

This is the study of ecosystems – how communities interact with each other and their habitat.

An aquarium as an example of an ecosystem

- Algae on the sides of the tank provide food for water snails.
- Water snails help to keep the water clear by eating algae.
- Water snails will need a supply of oxygen, so water plants will be needed to oxygenate the water as they carry out photosynthesis.
- If the growth of plants remains unchecked, they will eventually cover the surface of the water and so block out the light that is needed for photosynthesis.
- If there is no photosynthesis there will be no oxygen – water will become stale and unfit for animals.
- Clearly, the removal of the water would be a disaster for all animals and plants!

If the **correct proportion** of animals and plants is maintained, then the water conditions will be good enough to produce a **balanced ecosystem** – which will last and thrive.

Ecosystems which are not balanced soon disappear, providing immense problems for the communities which had existed in them.

Environment

This describes the **conditions** within an ecosystem.

These conditions are known as **environmental factors** and are made up of two parts:

(i) **Physical factors** (non-living factors) such as:

- amount of water
- light
- temperature
- pH (acidity/alkalinity)
- wind.

(ii) **Biological factors** – the effect of other living organisms in the habitat:

(a) **Predators/prey**. **Predators** eat other animals (**prey**).

(b) **Competitors**. Competition arises when animals and plants compete for space, water, minerals and light.

- Vegetable gardens are weeded to give crops maximum nutrients and space.
- Animals will compete for 'territory' and a space to live.

Adaptation

This refers to the features of animals and plants which enable them to live successfully in their **environment** or respond to **changes in their habitat**.

(i) **Adaptation in plants**

Grass has growing points very close to the ground, so when the lush green leaves are grazed by animals, or mowed by humans, the grass will grow again.

Cacti have no leaves in order to reduce water loss:

● they are able to store water and have very deep roots for times of drought

● they have spines to prevent animals eating them.

Pine needles are true leaves that are curled with the stomata on the inside to prevent water loss in the dry, windy conditions in which pine trees live.

(ii) **Adaptation in animals**

Polar bears and **penguins** have extra layers of fat to protect them from the sub-zero temperatures of the Arctic and Antarctic.

Camels in the desert have feet with a large surface area so they do not sink into soft sand. They can store a lot of water and lose very little water in sweat. Their sandy colour gives them good camouflage from predators in the desert.

Population

This refers to the numbers of organisms of the **same species**, which exist in a habitat.

How populations change in size

They will **increase** due to   (i)   birth of new individuals
(ii)   individuals moving **in (immigration)**.

They will **decrease** due to   (i)   death of individuals
(ii)   individuals moving **out (emigration)**.

Factors limiting population growth

1. **Food shortage**:

Food supplies need to increase as populations increase in order to avoid intense competition for dwindling food supplies.

2. **Shortage of space**:

Overcrowding leads to a quicker spread of disease, lack of living area and an increase in agitation and stress.

3. **Predation:**

Predators moving in will reduce numbers of individuals, slowing population growth.

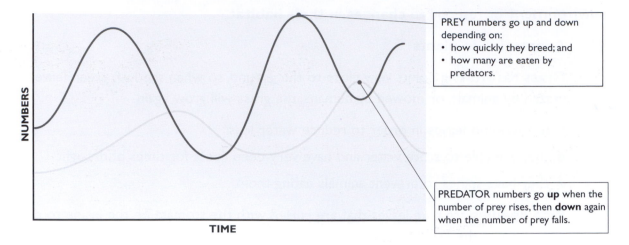

PREY numbers go up and down depending on:
- how quickly they breed; and
- how many are eaten by predators.

PREDATOR numbers go **up** when the number of prey rises, then **down** again when the number of prey falls.

4. **Increase of toxins (poisons)**

- Nitrogenous waste from animals will change into ammonia which is a poison to most animals.

- Increase of populations will cause a build up of toxins which will limit population growth.

- Man's effect on the environment increases toxins, for example:

    by the use of insecticides;

    by lead and mercury poisoning the environment;

    by the increased use of fertilizers – particularly nitrates, which become washed into rivers and streams causing algae to grow at a rapid rate which results in **unbalanced ecosystems**.

Measuring the size of a population using a quadrat

- Place quadrat on the ground.

- Count numbers of organisms of a particular species inside the quadrat – call this '**N**'.

- Count the number of quadrats used to study a particular area – call this '**Q**'.

Total population = N x Q

Food chains

Prey and predator form part of a **food chain** in which each organism provides the food for the next organism in the chain.

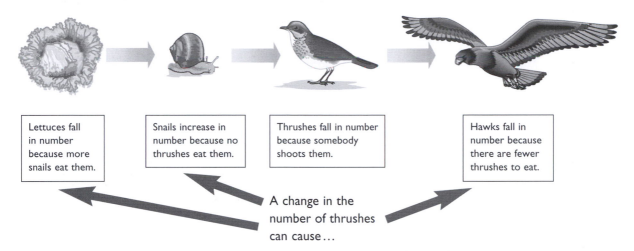

Lettuces fall in number because more snails eat them.

Snails increase in number because no thrushes eat them.

Thrushes fall in number because somebody shoots them.

Hawks fall in number because there are fewer thrushes to eat.

A change in the number of thrushes can cause...

In this food chain:

● **Lettuce** is the **primary producer**. The primary producer is **always a plant**.

● **Snail** is the **primary consumer**. The primary consumer is **always a herbivore**.

● **Thrush** is a **secondary consumer**. The secondary consumer is **always a carnivore**.

● **Hawk** is a **tertiary consumer** and is the **top carnivore** in this chain.

What do arrows in a food chain mean?

In simple terms, **A → B** means **A is eaten by B**.

● The arrow shows the **direction in which energy is transferred** in a food chain.

● Energy is lost to the environment – usually as heat – at every stage of a food chain, so only about 10% passes from one stage to the next.

Food webs

A food web is a set of **interconnected** food chains.

● This means that consumers have **more than one** supply of food.

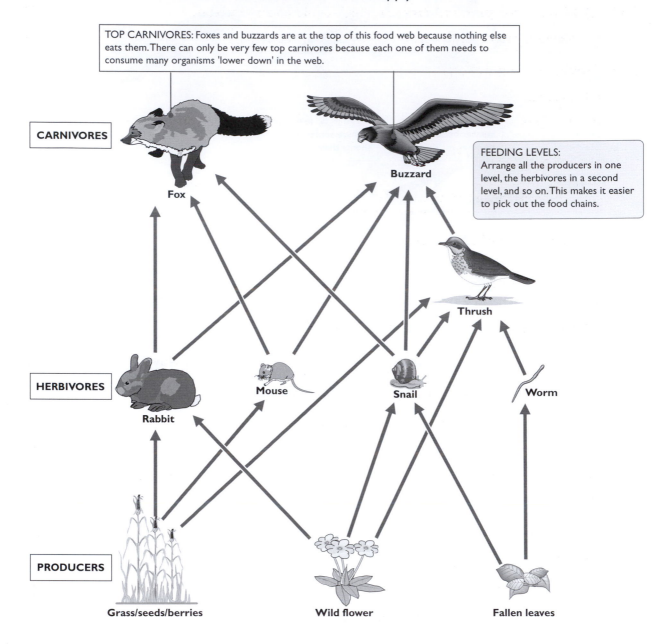

TOP CARNIVORES: Foxes and buzzards are at the top of this food web because nothing else eats them. There can only be very few top carnivores because each one of them needs to consume many organisms 'lower down' in the web.

CARNIVORES

Fox

Buzzard

FEEDING LEVELS:
Arrange all the producers in one level, the herbivores in a second level, and so on. This makes it easier to pick out the food chains.

Thrush

HERBIVORES

Rabbit

Mouse

Snail

Worm

PRODUCERS

Grass/seeds/berries

Wild flower

Fallen leaves

Decay is part of a food web

● When a body dies, the dead body is broken down by **decomposers** such as bacteria and fungi.

● Decomposers break down dead remains into simple chemicals such as **nitrates** that **enrich the soil**.

● Enriched soil enables plants (primary producers) to grow, thrive and support the food web.

Sample questions

Try these sample questions for yourself. The answers are given at the back of the book.

2.32 (a) Name three **physical factors** which could affect a habitat. (3)

(b) Name a **biological factor** which could affect a habitat. (1)

2.33 Explain how populations

(a) increase (2)

(b) decrease. (2)

2.34 Here are four typical food chains:

| lettuce → rabbit → fox → flea |

| oak tree → aphid → ladybird → robin |

| grass → earthworm → shrew → owl |

| algae → pond snail → leech → dragonfly nymph |

(a) Which food chain occurs in water? (1)

(b) Which food chain does not contain a vertebrate? (1)

(c) In which food chain is the herbivore a mammal? (1)

(d) Which food chain does not contain an insect? (1)

(e) In which food chain is the producer much larger than the herbivore? (1)

(f) In which food chain is the top carnivore a parasite? (1)

2.35 In a typical food chain:

(a) What is meant by the term 'decay'? (1)

(b) What type of organisms carry out decay? (1)

(c) Why is decay an important part of the food web? (2)

Summary

You should now know the following:

1. The main components of a cell and different specialised cells.

2. The main systems in the human body.

3. The various elements that make up our nutrition and what these are used for.

4. The different stages of digestion.

5. How humans move.

6. How humans reproduce.

7. What happens during respiration.

8. How humans breathe.

9. What is involved in leading a healthy lifestyle.

10. How we fight disease.

11. Photosynthesis and its part in increasing biomass.

12. That photosynthesis increases oxygen and decreases carbon dioxide in the air.

13. The process of photosynthesis, and how to test for presence of starch and oxygen.

14. What plants need to enable them to grow and be healthy.

15. The differences between organisms of the same species which is called variation.

16. About continuous and discontinuous variation.

17. Classification as the way we sort organisms into groups, e.g. the five kingdoms.

18. The differences between insects and spiders.

19. Features of the five classes of vertebrate animals.

20. That ecology is the study of the interaction of animals and plants.

21. The terms: *ecosystem; environment; environmental factors.*

22. How adaptation in animals and plants works.

23. How population increases and decreases, and factors limiting population growth.

24. Food chains and the relationship between predator and prey.

25. That the primary producer in a food chain is always a plant.

26. Carnivores and herbivores as different types of consumer.

27. That a food web is a set of interconnected food chains, and that decay is part of a food web.

Use the glossary at the back of the book for definitions of key words.

Test yourself

Before moving on to the next chapter, make sure you can answer the following questions. The answers are at the back of the book.

1. Draw diagrams of typical animal and plant cells and include labels for the following: **cell surface membrane**, **nucleus**, **cytoplasm**, **cellulose cell wall**, **central vacuole**, **chloroplasts** and **mitochondria**.

2. What do the following words describe: **tissue**, **organ**, **system**?

3. Humans need a diet containing carbohydrate, fat, mineral, protein and vitamins.

    (a) (i) In a balanced diet, which one of these gives us most of our energy?

    (ii) Name a food rich in this substance.

    (b) (i) Which one of these is used mainly for growth?

    (ii) Name a food rich in this substance.

4. List the main features of enzymes?

5. (a) What is a tendon?

    (b) What is a ligament?

6. Complete the following sentences:

    (a) Males and females develop reproductive organs during a stage of development called . . . .

    (b) The male gamete is the . . . . and this is produced in the . . . .

    (c) The female gamete is the . . . . and this is produced in the . . . .

    (d) Male and female gametes fuse together during fertilisation to form a . . . .

    (e) A fertilised egg, after cell division, settles in the thick lining of the uterus wall in a process called . . . .

    (f) Once the process in (e) has been completed, the mother is said to be . . . .

7. List the following organs in the correct order in which the air would meet them as we breathe in.

    bronchiole   air sac   mouth   bronchus   trachea

8. List two ways in which regular exercise is an essential part of healthy living.

9. Explain what photosynthesis is.

10. What are the raw materials needed for photosynthesis?

11. What are the products of photosynthesis?

12. What happens to the oxygen produced by photosynthesis?

13. What happens to the glucose produced by photosynthesis?

14. Nitrogen is present in all proteins; magnesium is needed to make chlorophyll.

    (a) Where will plants find supplies of these chemicals?

    (b) Which structures enable these chemicals to enter the plants?

15. Explain what the word **variation** means.

16. Give an example of a discontinuous variation in humans and say what this results from.

17. What does a scientist mean by the word 'classification'?

18. One man and his dog have much in common even though they are clearly different species. Say what they **do** have in common in terms of biological classification.

19. Name three features which are common to all arthropods.

20. Make a table with two headings, 'vertebrate' and 'invertebrate'. Put the following animals in the correct part of your table.

    earthworm   emu   shark   spider   whale   frog   crab   turtle   beetle   fox

21. Explain the terms

    (i) habitat;

    (ii) community.

22. What is an **ecosystem**?

23. What does the term **environment** mean?

24. What does the term **population** refer to?

25. List as many factors as you can which limit population growth.

26. Here is a simple food chain:

    rose → aphid → robin → cat

    (a) Which organism is the primary producer and why is it given this name?

    (b) Suggest two effects on the food chain of spraying the roses with insecticide.

27. (a) What is a food web?

    (b) Why is a food web different from a food chain?

CHEMISTRY

Chapter 3: 11+ Chemistry

3.1 Materials and their properties

Grouping and classifying materials

- The study of the materials which make up the world in which we live is called **chemistry**.

- Every material has two types of **properties** (features):

  (i) **Physical properties**.

  (ii) **Chemical properties**.

(i) Physical properties

ⓘ Physical properties are special to substances and may be observed and/or measured **without the substances changing into another substance**.

Some physical properties of materials

- **Hardness**:

  – If x makes a scratch on y, then x **is harder** than y.
  For example, diamond cannot be scratched by any other substance.

  – Hard materials **keep their shape** when hitting or being hit by other materials.
  For example, steel hammer heads, metal golf clubs, plastic safety helmets.

- **Strength**: ability to withstand loads without breaking or changing shape.

  For example, steel for buildings and railway tracks, fibre glass for boats.

- **Flexibility**: can be bent or twisted.

  For example, wood for archery bows, string, rope, copper wire.

- **Magnetic behaviour**: can be attracted to magnets.

  For example, iron and steel are magnetic (aluminium, copper and non-metals are not).

- **Conductivity**:

  – **conductors** let heat and/or electricity pass through them.
  For example, all metals.

  – **Insulators** do **not** let heat/electricity pass through them.
  For example, wood, plastics, air, expanded polystyrene.

(ii) Chemical properties

ⓘ Chemical properties describe the composition of a substance and how it changes into another substance. When this happens, a **chemical reaction** takes place.

Sample questions

Try this sample question for yourself. The answers are given at the back of the book.

3.1   Suggest which physical property each of the following descriptions refer to and give **one** example of a material that fits each description.

(a) Can be bent or twisted.   (2)

(b) Can let heat and/or electricity pass through it.   (2)

(c) Can keep its shape when hit and cannot be scratched.   (2)

(d) Can withstand loads without breaking or changing shape.   (2)

3.2 Types of soils

- Rocks are broken down into small particles by a process call **weathering**.

- Rock particles are changed into fertile soil by the addition of **humus** (decayed plant and animal remains that add nutrients and help keep the soil moist).

- Large rock particles have spaces between them which allow good drainage, e.g. sandy soil.

- Tiny rock particles do not have much space between them and are easily waterlogged, e.g. clay soil.

Sandy soils – not very good for growth of most plants

- Large spaces between particles for air and water.

- Good drainage, hardly ever become waterlogged.

- Dry out quickly and minerals easily washed away.

Clay soils – not very good for growth of most plants

- Very tiny spaces between particles for air and water.

- Poor drainage, often become waterlogged.

- Lack of a good supply of air resulting in poor root growth.

- Very little humus to provide nutrients for good plant growth.

Loam soils – ideal for good plant growth

- Mixture of sand and clay particles with plenty of humus.

- Good drainage at a slower rate than in sandy soil.

- Plenty of air spaces for good root growth.

- Attracts underground animals which helps maintain a good amount of humus.

- Retains minerals.

Sample questions

Try these sample questions for yourself. The answers are given at the back of the book.

3.2 Which process breaks rocks down into smaller pieces? (1)

3.3 What do you know about the size of particles and their effect on drainage in
(a) sandy soils; (b) clay soils? (2)

3.3 Solids, liquids and gases

ⓘ Solids, liquids and gases are known as the three **states of matter**.

A particular amount (**mass**) of a substance in each of the three states will show the following features (**properties**):

	Solid	Liquid	Gas
Mass	Fixed	Fixed	Fixed
Volume	Fixed	Fixed	Changes*
Shape	Fixed	Changes*	Changes*

* Liquids and gases are called **fluids** because they can change shape and flow.

ⓘ All matter is made up from particles which are moving all the time.

- In a **fluid** the movement is from one place to another.

- In a **solid** the movement is in **one** place in the form of vibrations.

Particles in solids

● Packed closely together (regular patterns in crystals).

● Held together strongly by various forces, so particles can only vibrate where they are and not move around. This is why a solid keeps its shape.

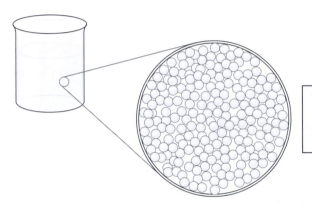

Particles in a solid are fixed in a pattern, so you cannot change its volume or easily change its shape.

Particles in liquids

● Particles are close together so a liquid cannot be squashed, i.e. its volume remains the same.

● Particles are constantly moving around each other as they are not held together as strongly as in a solid, so a liquid is able to flow from one place to another.

● A liquid will change shape and match the shape of the container it is in even though the amount of liquid (**volume**) remains the same if it is put into different containers.

The particles in a liquid move around each other. There is no pattern.

Particles in a gas

● Particles move around rapidly in all directions and so a gas will completely fill any container.

● The big spaces between particles make it relatively easy to squash a gas into a smaller space (reduce its volume). This brings the particles closer together and it is possible to squash the particles so close together that the gas becomes a liquid.

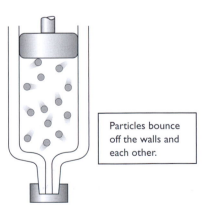

Particles bounce off the walls and each other.

Particles can be squeezed closer together.

3.4 Changing materials

There are two types of change:

(i) Physical change:

● Substances do **not** change into other substances, i.e. there is **no chemical reaction** (e.g. when salt crystals dissolve in water).

● Substances may **change state** (e.g. butter changes from solid to liquid as it melts).

● Changes are **temporary** and may be reversed (e.g. salt crystals are returned when water is evaporated or liquid butter will change to solid as it cools).

(ii) Chemical change:

● Substances change into **different** substances as a result of a **chemical reaction**.

● In most cases the change is **permanent** and cannot be reversed.

(i) Physical change

Heating and cooling

● Adding energy to a substance makes it hotter.

● Removing energy from a substance makes it cooler.

ⓘ **Temperature** is the measure of how hot or cold a substance is.

● Temperature is measured using a **thermometer** marked with a scale in degrees **Celsius** (°C) (originally called the centigrade scale because there are 100 degrees between the boiling and freezing points of water).

Boiling point and melting point

The temperature at which a liquid changes into a gas is called the **boiling point**.

- The boiling point of pure water is 100 °C.

- The process of changing a liquid into a gas is called **evaporation**.

- The process of changing a gas into a liquid is called **condensation**.

- **Both** of these processes take place at the **boiling point** of the substance.

Temporary changes

The water cycle: the processes of evaporation and condensation

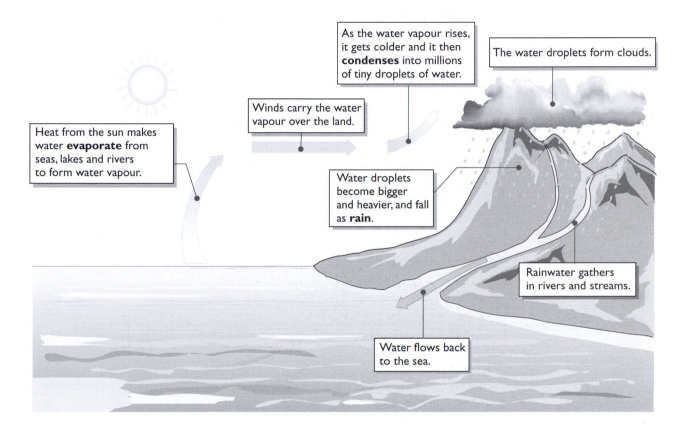

As the water vapour rises, it gets colder and it then **condenses** into millions of tiny droplets of water.

The water droplets form clouds.

Winds carry the water vapour over the land.

Heat from the sun makes water **evaporate** from seas, lakes and rivers to form water vapour.

Water droplets become bigger and heavier, and fall as **rain**.

Rainwater gathers in rivers and streams.

Water flows back to the sea.

The temperature at which a liquid changes into a solid is called the **melting point** (or freezing point).

- The freezing point of pure water is 0 °C.

- The process of changing a solid into a liquid is called **melting**.

- The process of changing a liquid into a solid is called **freezing**.

- **Both** of these processes take place at the **melting point** of the substance.

Changes of state

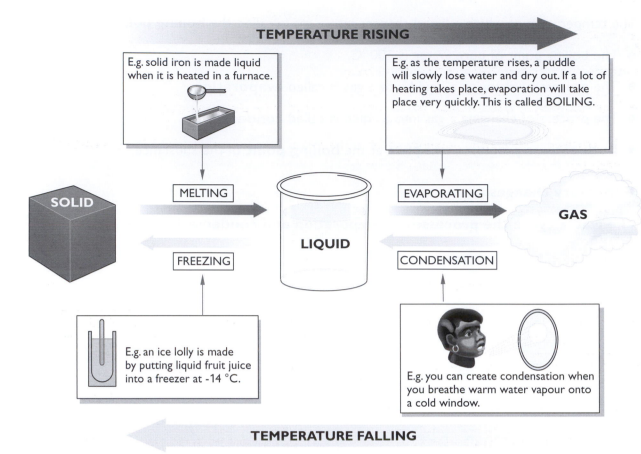

TEMPERATURE RISING

E.g. solid iron is made liquid when it is heated in a furnace.

E.g. as the temperature rises, a puddle will slowly lose water and dry out. If a lot of heating takes place, evaporation will take place very quickly. This is called BOILING.

SOLID

MELTING

LIQUID

EVAPORATING

GAS

FREEZING

CONDENSATION

E.g. an ice lolly is made by putting liquid fruit juice into a freezer at -14 °C.

E.g. you can create condensation when you breathe warm water vapour onto a cold window.

TEMPERATURE FALLING

Using boiling and melting points to see if a substance is pure

● Each substance has its own boiling point and melting point.

● Adding impurities raises the boiling point and lowers the freezing points of substances.

For example:

– Adding salt to water makes it boil at a temperature higher than 100 °C and freeze below 0 °C. This is why salt is spread on roads when frost is forecast.

– Water expands when it freezes (helps to break rocks into smaller pieces), but this expansion can also break water pipes, which is why motorists will add antifreeze to the water in their cars during winter and householders insulate pipes in the roof.

(ii) Chemical change

ⓘ A chemical change means a **new** substance has been made.

Chemical changes NOT NEEDING heat

- | air (oxygen) + water + iron (solid metal) | → | rust (useless powder) |

  To **stop** this reaction happening, water and air (oxygen) are **prevented from contact** with the iron by covering it with a coat of:

  – oil

  – zinc (galvanising)

  – paint

  – plastic

  – tin (as in tins containing food)

- | vinegar + bicarbonate of soda | → | fizzing + new substance + gas (carbon dioxide) |

- | small stones + sand + cement + water | → | concrete (hard solid) |

Chemical changes NEEDING heat

- **Cooking food** causes a new substance that cannot be changed back. For example:
  – Frying/boiling an egg.
  – Baking dough (flour + water + yeast + sugar) to make bread.

- **Burning**.

  ⓘ Heating is **not** the same as burning.

  – The two are often confused, as heating can **sometimes** lead to burning.
  – Burning happens when a substance is hot enough to react with **oxygen** (from the air) to form new substances.
  – Burning releases **more energy** (heat, light, sound) than is needed to start it.

Some important burning reactions

General reaction:

| fuel + oxygen (from air) + heat | → | ash + gases + energy |

Fossil fuels:

- **Coal**: a solid fuel that burns to form ash + gases + energy.

- **Oil** (which produces petrol, wax): a liquid that burns to form gases + energy.

- **Natural gas**: a gas that burns to form other gases + energy.

11+

C

The reactions:

- fuel (wood/coal) + oxygen + heat → ash + carbon dioxide + water + energy (heat, light)

- fuel (oil/natural gas) + oxygen + heat → carbon dioxide + water + energy (heat, light)

- wax (candle) + oxygen + heat → carbon dioxide + water + energy (heat, light)

(i) Two important facts about fossil fuels:

1. They are **non-renewable**: cannot be used again and there is a **limited supply**.

2. Burning causes **pollution** by releasing ash and gases into the air.

All fuels release carbon dioxide (a greenhouse gas) into the air.

Solid fuels, e.g. coal, release ash (as smoke) and gases (e.g. sulphur dioxide) which produce acid rain (harmful to living things).

Sample questions

Try these sample questions for yourself. The answers are given at the back of the book.

3.6   In each case, give the name of the process which best describes the changes below:

(a) solid → liquid (1)

(b) liquid → gas (1)

(c) liquid → solid (1)

(d) gas → liquid (1)

3.7   The changes which are listed in question 3.6 are physical changes. List at least two features of a physical change. (2)

3.8   Pure water boils at 100 °C and freezes at 0 °C.

(a) What happens to the boiling point when salt is added to water? (1)

(b) Why do local councils often put salt on the roads in winter? (2)

3.9   (a) Iron (the only metal to rust) needs two substances to change it into rust. What are they? (2)

(b) List three ways of preventing iron from rusting. (3)

(c) Why is rusting not a useful chemical reaction? (2)

3.10 | candle wax   coal   natural gas   oil   peat   wood |

(a) Which of the above are fossil fuels? (3)

(b) Which of the fuels burn completely to form gases only? (3)

(c) Which two things are needed (apart from the fuel) for it to be able to burn? (2)

(d) Why is burning fuels harmful to the environment? (2)

3.5 Separating mixtures of materials

● Separating mixtures involves **physical processes**, i.e. no chemical change takes place.

● There needs to be something that one part of the mixture does that the other does not.

Mixture	Action	What happens	Physical differences
Sand + sawdust	Add water	Sand sinks; sawdust floats	Densities
Sand + iron filings	Use a magnet	Iron sticks to magnet; sand does not	Magnetic attraction
Sand + salt	Add water	Salt dissolves; sand does not	Solubility

Dissolving

● Blue copper sulphate crystals will 'disappear' in water to form a clear, blue liquid.

● We say the copper sulphate has **dissolved** in the water to form a blue **solution**.

● Substances which dissolve in liquids are called **soluble substances**.

● Substances which **do not** dissolve in liquids are called **insoluble substances**.

● A **solution** is a mixture of a soluble substance (called the **solute**) which is broken up and spread evenly throughout the liquid (called the **solvent**).

● In other words, the **solvent** (e.g. water) dissolves the **solute** (e.g. salt) to form the **solution** (e.g. salt solution).

● Substances will dissolve more rapidly in warm water than in cold water.

● Small crystals or powders will dissolve more easily than large crystals.

Solubility

● This term describes how well a substance dissolves, i.e. how **much** solid dissolves in a **particular amount** of liquid (solvent).

● The solubility of a substance may be increased by:
  – heating;
  – stirring.

Sieving

● Used to separate two/more solids with different sized particles.

● A sieve is a tray with holes in it called a mesh. A fine mesh has small holes so will only let small particles go through it.

- Examples of sieves:
    - A tea strainer holds back the tea leaves whilst allowing the clear liquid to pass through.
    - A gardener will separate stones from soil by using a sieve. Stones are held in the mesh, whilst the smaller soil particles fall through.

Filtering

- Used to separate **insoluble solids** from liquids.

- Only **solutions** and **pure solvents** can pass through filter paper.

- **Residue**: the insoluble solid left in the filter paper, e.g. mud from muddy water.

- **Filtrate**: the liquid that passes through the filter paper, e.g. solutions and pure liquids.

Decanting

Another way of separating **insoluble solids** from liquids.

- Insoluble solids sink and settle at the bottom of the liquid as sediment.

- Clear liquid is gently poured off leaving the undisturbed sediment behind.

Evaporating

⚠ Evaporating is the **only** way of removing the solvent from a solution.

- As a solution is heated the liquid (**solvent**) changes into a gas (**evaporates**).

- When the liquid has evaporated, the dissolved solid (**solute**) is left behind.

Sample questions

Try these sample questions for yourself. The answers are given at the back of the book.

3.11 You have a mixture of sulphur (a yellow solid) and hydrated copper sulphate (blue crystals). Sulphur is insoluble in water. Hydrated copper sulphate is soluble in water.

    (a) What do the words **soluble** and **insoluble** mean? (2)

    (b) What happens when you add water to your mixture? (2)

    (c) If you filter the mixture after adding water, which substance is (i) the residue; (ii) the filtrate? (2)

3.12 Copy out and complete the following sentences.

    (a) A sieve is used to separate two/more . . . . with . . . . sized particles. (2)

    (b) Filtering is used to separate . . . . solids from . . . . (2)

    (c) Insoluble solids . . . . and settle at the bottom as sediment. (1)

    (d) Gently pouring off clear liquid leaving the sediment behind is called . . . . (1)

3.13 Write out the following sentences, completing them by using the words listed below.

| evaporated | solute | solvent |

    (a) When a solution is heated, the liquid (called the . . . .) changes into a gas. (1)

    (b) When the liquid has . . . . , the . . . . is left behind. (2)

Summary

You should now know the following:

1.   How materials are classified according to their physical properties.

2.   The different types of soil and their main features.

3.   The main features of the states of matter.

4.   Physical and chemical changes in materials.

5.   How to separate different mixtures of materials.

Use the glossary at the back of the book for definitions of key words.

Test yourself

Before moving on to the next chapter, make sure you can answer the following questions. The answers are at the back of the book.

1. (a) What do physical properties describe?

   (b) What do chemical properties describe?

2. What is humus?

3.

Substance	A	B	C
Melting point (°C)	−73	−7	649
Boiling point (°C)	−10	59	1107

If room temperature is 20°C, which substance is (a) a solid; (b) a liquid; (c) a gas?

4. List two features of a chemical change.

5. Study the chemical reaction and answer the questions below:

   | blue powder + water | → | ink |

   Which of these three is (a) the solution; (b) the solvent; (c) the solute?

Chapter 4: 13+ Chemistry

4.1 A further look at classifying materials

Substances – also known as matter

- All substances are made from tiny particles called **atoms**.

- There are about 100 different types of atom.

- The word 'atom' comes from the Greek word *atomos* (indivisible).

- Atoms join together to form **molecules**.

- Substances can be put into three main groups: **solids**, **liquids**, **gases**. These groups are known as the **three states of matter**.

- Most substances can exist in all three states, they can change from one to another by a **change in temperature**.

ⓘ There is no change in mass when a substance changes state.

Heating a substance causes the particles to:

- Move faster, i.e. have **greater kinetic energy**.

- Move further apart: so the substance becomes bigger (increases its volume). The substance **expands**.

ⓘ Heating – no change in mass, but increasing volume, results in the **density decreasing**.

Cooling a substance causes the particles to:

- Move more slowly, i.e. have **less kinetic energy**.

- Move more closely together: volume decreases.

ⓘ Cooling – no change in mass, but decreasing volume, results in the **density increasing**.

The **expansion** of liquids, e.g. **mercury** and **alcohol**, when they are **heated** and their **contraction** when they are **cooled** are used in thermometers.

- The **melting point** is the temperature at which a:
  - Solid changes to a liquid.
  - Liquid changes to a solid – also known as **freezing**.

- The **boiling point** is the temperature at which a:
  - Liquid changes to a gas – i.e. **evaporates**.
  - Gas changes to a liquid – i.e. **condenses**.

ⓘ **Each substance has its own boiling and melting points.** This fact can be used to (i) identify a substance; (ii) determine if it is pure or not.

Changing state

⚗ Generally, for most substances:

    Adding heat: **solid → liquid → gas**

    Removing heat (cooling):   **gas → liquid → solid**

Sublimation

Some substances, e.g. **carbon dioxide** and **iodine**, miss out the liquid state when they are heated or cooled. This is called **sublimation**.

    Adding heat: **solid → gas**

    Removing heat (cooling):   **gas → solid**

Types of substance

There are two main groups: pure substances and impure substances.

ⓘ **Pure substances**: contain **one** substance only. This group is made up of **elements** and **compounds**.

Impure substances: contain **two or more** substances and are called **mixtures**.

(i) Pure substances – elements and compounds

(A) Elements

- Elements are **single substances** which are the building blocks of all matter.

- There are about 100 elements and they are all listed in the **Periodic Table**.

- The smallest particle of an element is an **atom** of that element. The chemical symbol for each element, e.g. C for carbon, represents **one atom** of carbon.

- Elements are materials which are made up of **one type of atom**, so there are about 100 different types of atom.

Structure of atoms

This section is not examined at Common Entrance but is included for information. Note, however, that some chemical symbols are required knowledge. Those in **bold** on the Periodic Table will be examined.

Every atom consists of a nucleus which is **positively** charged, surrounded by a cloud of electrons which are **negatively** charged.

There are three main types of particle in an atom:

(i) **Protons**: positively charged particles. The number of these is called the **atomic number** of that element.

(ii) **Neutrons**: a particle found also in the nucleus which has mass but **no** electric charge.

(iii) **Electrons**: negatively charged particles with much smaller mass than protons which move around the nucleus.

ⓘ All atoms are electrically neutral, so: **number of protons = number of electrons**

The Periodic Table

● This is a list of all the elements listed in the order of their atomic number. Note that the chemical symbols used on the Periodic Table represent one atom of each of the elements. The diagram below shows a small selection of those elements.

● The horizontal rows are called **periods**.

● The table was drawn up in 1869 by a Russian chemistry teacher called **Dimitri Mendeléev**.

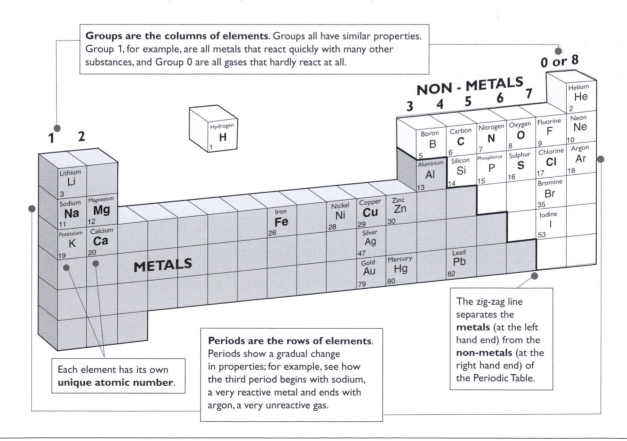

Groups are the columns of elements. Groups all have similar properties. Group 1, for example, are all metals that react quickly with many other substances, and Group 0 are all gases that hardly react at all.

Each element has its own **unique atomic number.**

Periods are the rows of elements. Periods show a gradual change in properties; for example, see how the third period begins with sodium, a very reactive metal and ends with argon, a very unreactive gas.

The zig-zag line separates the **metals** (at the left hand end) from the **non-metals** (at the right hand end) of the Periodic Table.

Metals and non-metals

Look at the Periodic Table and note the diagonal line towards the right that divides the table into two major groups: **metals** and **non-metals**.

ⓘ **Metals are:**

- **All solid** at room temperature (except mercury – a liquid).

- **Shiny.**

- **Bendy**: can be bent, twisted or pulled out into wires.

- **Conduct electricity and heat**, i.e. are **conductors**.

- Able to combine with **oxygen** (during burning) to form **solid oxides** called **bases**.

- **All** bases will neutralise acids to form **salts**.

- **Some** bases will dissolve in water to form **alkalis**.

ⓘ **Non-metals are:**

- **Solid**: carbon, iodine, silicon, sulphur.

  Liquid: bromine.

  Gas: oxygen, nitrogen, chlorine.

- **Dull**.

- **Brittle**: snap and break into powder.

- Most do **not** conduct electricity and heat, i.e. are **insulators**.

- Able to combine with **oxygen** (during burning) to form **oxides** which dissolve in water to form **acids**.

Hydrogen – a special case

- Has **physical properties of a non-metal** (gas, non-conductor of electricity and heat).

- Has **chemical properties of a metal** (most acids are compounds of hydrogen).

- Has **atomic number of 1**, i.e. has a nucleus of **one proton**.

- Has the **smallest atom** and **lowest density** of all the elements.

- Is normally placed just outside the main body of the Periodic Table at the top.

- Combines with **oxygen** (during burning) to form a **liquid oxide** (water), which is **neutral**.

(B) Compounds

When two or more elements combine as a result of a **chemical reaction**, then a compound is formed.

- Compounds are **entirely different in all respects** from the elements which reacted to form it.

- Compounds are represented by formulae showing the atoms that make up each molecule, e.g. H_2O is the formula for a water molecule which is made from two atoms of hydrogen and one atom of oxygen.

Other important formulae are:

CO_2	–	carbon dioxide
O_2	–	oxygen gas
CH_4	–	methane
$NaCl$	–	sodium chloride
HCl	–	hydrochloric acid
$NaOH$	–	sodium hydroxide
$CaCO_3$	–	calcium carbonate

- The substance(s) with which you start is/are called the **reactant(s)**.

- The substance(s) produced as a result of a chemical reaction is/are called the **product(s)**.

Two important features of all chemical reactions

ⓘ 1. Elements which are present as reactants will **also be present** in the product(s). They could well be in a different combination or form, but they **will be there**.

2. **The total mass of reactant(s) = the total mass of product(s)**.

- When compounds are **formed**, a **combining reaction** has taken place.

- The reactant **gains mass**. For example, magnesium (a silver metal) burns in air (combines with oxygen – a colourless gas) to form the compound magnesium oxide (a white solid).

- We show the reaction in the form of a **word equation** with an arrow '→' which means 'goes to form'.

$$\boxed{\text{magnesium (s) + oxygen (g)}} \rightarrow \boxed{\text{magnesium oxide (s)}}$$

The small letters in brackets are **state symbols** which describe the physical state of substances:

(s) – solid;   (l) – liquid;   (g) – gas   (aq) – aqueous solution*

*An aqueous solution is where a substance has been dissolved or diluted in water

- When compounds are **split up**, a **decomposing reaction** has taken place.

- The reactant **loses mass**. For example, heating blue crystals of hydrated copper sulphate will produce a white powder (anhydrous copper sulphate) plus invisible gas (water vapour).

| hydrated copper sulphate (s) + heat | → | anhydrous copper sulphate (s) + water (g) |

- When heating white powdered limestone (calcium carbonate) a white powder (calcium oxide) will be produced. At first, it looks as if nothing has happened, but when the limestone is weighed, the resulting calcium oxide will show that a loss in mass has taken place. This is because when the calcium carbonate is heated, the invisible gas carbon dioxide is given off.

| calcium carbonate (s) + heat | → | calcium oxide (s) + carbon dioxide (g) |

- Carbon dioxide dissolves in water to form the weak acid **carbonic acid**.

| carbon dioxide (g) + water (l) | → | carbonic acid (aq) |

- Carbonic acid reacts with limestone (calcium carbonate) which is often used in buildings. This reaction with the limestone is a process called **weathering**.

| carbonic acid (aq) + calcium carbonate (s) | → | calcium hydrogen carbonate (aq) + carbon dioxide (g) |

(ii) Impure substances – mixtures

- These are two or more substances that are put together **without a chemical reaction having taken place**.

Some examples of mixtures

Name of mixture	What is mixed
Any solution	Solute + solvent
Any dilute acid	Concentrated acid (solute) + water (solvent)
Blue ink	Blue powder (solute) + water (solvent)
Sea water	Salt and many chemicals (solute) + water (solvent)
Concrete	Sand + cement + small stones + water
Air	Nitrogen + oxygen + carbon dioxide + water vapour

Composition of air – a mixture of colourless gases

Gas	Approximate % by volume
Nitrogen	78%
Oxygen	20%
Noble gases (mainly argon)	1%
Carbon dioxide	0.04%
Water vapour (responsible for **humidity**)	Varies according to location
Impurities (e.g. sulphur dioxide, smoke emissions)	Varies according to location

Nitrogen – the main gas in the air (78%) – is:

- An **element**.
- A fairly unreactive gas at room temperature.
- Used as a raw material to make other chemicals, e.g. fertilisers.
- Liquid nitrogen is used in large quantities to freeze foods.

Oxygen – the gas of life, fire and rusting (20%) – is:

- An **element**.
- The **only** colourless gas that re-lights a glowing splint.
- Reasonably soluble in water (think of the fishes!) to form a neutral solution.
- A reactive gas: responsible for burning, rusting and respiration in living things.

Carbon dioxide – a 'greenhouse gas' which is vital to the well being of plants (0.03%) – is:

- A **compound**.
- More dense than air.
- The **only** gas which turns clear **limewater chalky**.
- Used by plants as a raw material for **photosynthesis**.
- Released into the air by (i) burning of fuels; (ii) being a waste product of **respiration**.
- Soluble in water to form a weak acid – rainwater is always **slightly** acidic.
- Responsible for the **greenhouse effect**. It traps some of the heat within the atmosphere which would otherwise radiate back into space. This causes the air and the earth to warm (**global warming**) because the constant input of heat from the Sun is now greater than the amount of heat radiating away from the Earth into space. The atmosphere works like a greenhouse which is designed to trap heat inside it.

Water vapour (variable amount in air) is:

- A neutral compound.

- Responsible for the **humidity** of the atmosphere.

- A colourless liquid which freezes at 0°C and boils at 100°C – these temperatures are tests of the **purity** of water.

- Able to combine with oxygen to cause **rusting** of iron.

- Used by plants as a raw material for **photosynthesis**.

- Released into the air by (i) burning of fuels; (ii) being a waste product of **respiration**; (iii) **evaporation** of water from the sea, rivers, lakes and ponds.

⚗ Two chemical tests to show that **water is present**

(i) Turns **white** anhydrous copper sulphate **blue**.

(ii) Turns **blue** cobalt chloride paper **pink**.

Separating mixtures

ⓘ Separation merely puts parts of mixtures in different places – there is **no chemical reaction**.

- The **method** of separation used depends upon **which part of the mixture you want to keep**.

⚗ **To increase the solubility of a substance:**

- **Heat it**: the activity of molecules increases as energy is added.

- **Break big chunks into smaller pieces (powder)**: this increases the **surface area** for the solvent to act upon.

- **Stir it**: this will increase the surface area of the solute by spreading it around.

Saturated solution

- This is a solution which has the maximum amount of solute dissolved in it at a particular temperature. Remember solubility increases as the temperature rises.

- **Undissolved solid** on the bottom of a beaker will tell you that the solution is **saturated**.

Methods of separation

- **Sieving**: separates two/more solids with different sized particles.

- **Filtering**: separates insoluble solids from liquids.

⚠ **Remember**: only **solutions** and **pure solvents** can pass through filter paper. Insoluble solids are left as **residue** on the filter paper.

- **Decanting**: separates liquids from insoluble solids.

- **Evaporating**: the **only** way of removing the solvent from a solution – normally used to recover and keep the **solute**.

- **Distillation**: used to recover the **solvent** from a solution. This process is in two parts:

  (i) **Evaporation**: to remove the solvent as a vapour from the solution.

  (ii) **Condensation**: to change the solvent vapour into pure solvent.

  If **one** liquid is recovered, the process is called **simple distillation**. If **two/more** liquids are recovered, the process is called **fractional distillation**.

Simple distillation

The water cooled (Liebig) condenser has two main features:

(i) The condensing tube is kept cool by an outer tube containing cold water moving in the **opposite** direction to the hot vapour flow.

(ii) The condensing tube slopes down towards the collecting tube (or flask).

Simple distillation

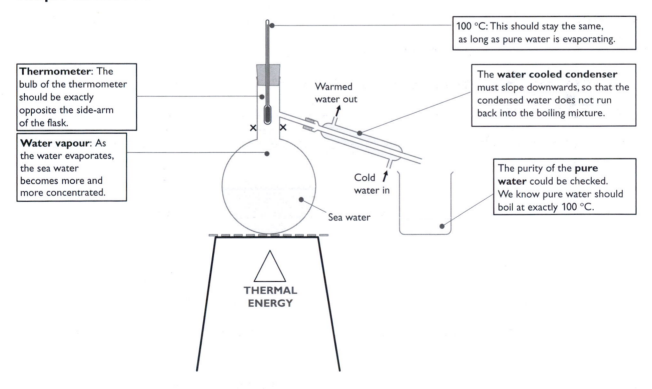

Thermometer: The bulb of the thermometer should be exactly opposite the side-arm of the flask.

Water vapour: As the water evaporates, the sea water becomes more and more concentrated.

Warmed water out

Cold water in

Sea water

THERMAL ENERGY

100 °C: This should stay the same, as long as pure water is evaporating.

The **water cooled condenser** must slope downwards, so that the condensed water does not run back into the boiling mixture.

The purity of the **pure water** could be checked. We know pure water should boil at exactly 100 °C.

Fractional distillation

This process uses the principle that **each liquid has its own boiling point**.
For example:

- The ethanol (boiling point 78°C) can be separated from the water (boiling point 100°C) in wine.

- Crude oil is a mixture of many liquids that are separated by fractional distillation.

● **Chromatography is used to separate mixtures of two or more soluble substances**.

This method depends upon the physical property of **solubility**.

- **Each substance has its own solubility**, i.e. some solids dissolve better than others.

- The solvent will move up chromatography paper (like filter paper) and will take the dissolved solids with it.

- The chromatography paper tries to absorb the solids and 'hold them back'.

- Solids will stop at some point on the paper, whilst the solvent continues to travel upwards.

- **The solid which dissolves best, travels the furthest**, i.e. stops at the highest point on the paper.

- Chromatography is used for analysis of small quantities of mixtures. It will often be used by:

  • Food chemists: to determine the additives and ingredients in foodstuffs, e.g. the colourings in sweets.

  • Police: to match up samples from a suspect to substances found at a crime scene.

  • Biochemists: to separate proteins into their various parts in the constant search for drugs to cure illnesses.

Sample questions

Try these sample questions for yourself. The answers are given at the back of the book.

4.1 Draw a table with the headings 'elements', 'compounds' and 'mixtures'.
Put the following substances into the correct columns: (12)

> air   carbon   carbon dioxide   distilled water   sea water   iron filings   crude oil
> dilute sulphuric acid   magnesium   oxygen   sodium chloride   iron sulphide

4.2 Make a table with three headings 'metal element', 'non-metal element' and 'compound'.
Put the following substances into the correct part of your table: (10)

> carbon   copper sulphate   iron filings   magnesium   mercury   oxygen
> sodium   sulphur   water   zinc oxide

4.3 Select the 'odd one out' in each of the following groups and suggest why you have made this choice.

(a) Copper, iron, mercury, zinc. (2)

(b) Copper, iron, lead, sodium. (2)

(c) Carbon dioxide, copper oxide, nitrogen oxide, sulphur dioxide. (2)

(d) Carbon, iron, sulphur, zinc. (2)

4.4 *Heating* a substance can *cause* a *chemical reaction* to take place. For example, a *reactant* may *decompose* into two *products*. What do the words in italics mean? (5)

4.5 (a) What evidence would you look for to show that a combining reaction had taken place? (2)

(b) Choose an example of a combining reaction and write a word equation that describes this. (5)

4.6 Dry air has the following composition:

78% gas A

20% gas B

2% other gases

(a) What is (i) gas A; (ii) gas B? (1)

(b) Name one of the other gases. (1)

(c) (i) What is the gas that is responsible for the **humidity** of the air. (1)

(ii) Describe a chemical test to identify this gas. (2)

13+
C

4.7 Copy out the table and complete it to suggest whether the processes listed cause the amounts of nitrogen, oxygen and carbon dioxide to increase, decrease or remain the same. (15)

Process	Nitrogen	Oxygen	Carbon dioxide
Burning a fossil fuel			
Photosynthesis			
Respiration			
Passing air through limewater			
Rusting			

4.8 (a) Draw a labelled diagram to show how you would **best** obtain some pure water from a sample of sea water. (6)

(b) How would you test that the water you had obtained was pure? (2)

4.9 What method would you use to:

(a) Recover solid salt from salt solution? (1)

(b) Recover mud from muddy water? (1)

(c) Find out how many pigments there were in black felt-tipped pen ink? (1)

(d) Recover the alcohol from a small glass of wine? (1)

4.2 Indicators, acids and alkalis

Indicators

These are substances that change their appearance (e.g. colour) when they come in contact with particular substances.

They **indicate** that a particular substance is present.

Indicators you know about already

> (i) **Limewater**: changes from **clear** to **chalky** to show **carbon dioxide** is present.
>
> **Anhydrous copper sulphate**: changes from **white** to **blue** to show **water** is present.
>
> **Anhydrous cobalt chloride**: changes from **blue** to **pink** to show **water** is present.

Indicators to show that liquids are either acid or alkali or neutral

Litmus

- Litmus is extracted from a type of lichen plant and forms a purple solution in water.

> (i) **Purple** litmus solution will turn **red** when it is added to **acids**.
>
> **Purple** litmus solution will turn **blue** when it is added to **alkalis**.
>
> **Purple** litmus solution **does not change colour** when it is added to **neutral** liquids.

Litmus is used in the laboratory in three different forms:

1. As a purple solution of the dye in water.

2. As **red** test papers to detect alkalis and neutral liquids.

3. As **blue** test papers to detect acids and neutral liquids.

Testing 'strength' of acids/alkalis – the pH scale

- The pH scale runs from 0 to 14.

- The middle of the scale is 7 and **all liquids with a pH of 7 are neutral**.

- Solutions which have a pH **less than 7** are **acids**.

- Solutions which have a pH **more than 7** are **alkalis**.

- Weak acids/alkalis have pH values close to the mid-point (7).

  For example, a range of 5–8 includes:

  – 'Natural' acids found in foods: vinegar, citrus fruits (pH 5–7).

  – 'Weak' alkalis: detergents, indigestion medicine, baking powder (pH 7–9).

- Strong acids/alkalis have pH values close to the end points (0 and 14).

  For example:

  – Sulphuric, hydrochloric acids (pH 0–4).

  – Sodium, calcium hydroxides (pH 10–14).

pH values can be determined by using (i) Universal Indicator; (ii) a pH probe.

Universal Indicator (UI)

This is a mixture of plant dyes and is available as (i) a green liquid; (ii) test papers. The indicator will change colour for different pH values.

pH Scale

0	1	2	3	4	5	6	7	8	9	10	11	12	13	14
pink	red			orange	yellow		green		blue			purple		

See *So you really want to learn Science Book 2*, page 179 to see the colour changes.

Neutralisation

Acids are able to 'cancel' out alkalis in a chemical reaction known as **neutralisation**. For example, sodium hydroxide is a strong alkali – purple with UI added. Hydrochloric acid (hydrogen chloride) is a strong acid – red with UI added. Add the acid slowly to the alkali until the neutral point is reached – UI turns green.

The resulting solution will be (i) warmer; (ii) a neutral solution of sodium chloride (**a salt**), dissolved in water.

The word equation to describe the chemical reaction that has happened is:

hydrochloric acid + sodium hydroxide	→	sodium chloride + water

acid + alkali	→	**salt + water**

The water can be evaporated from the sodium chloride solution to leave crystals of solid sodium chloride.

- Lime is an alkali which is used to treat acid soils, acid indigestion and to manufacture fertilizer.

Diluting acids with water

- Adding water to acids does **not substantially change** the pH of the acid – it merely dilutes the acid.

- Concentrated acids are made dilute by **slowly adding small quantities** of concentrated acid to **large quantities** of water.

More about salts

Acids

These are all compounds of hydrogen and it is the **acid** which gives a salt its **second name**.

Name of acid	Chemical name	Second name of salts produced
Hydrochloric acid	Hydrogen chloride	-chloride
Sulphuric acid	Hydrogen sulphate	-sulphate
Nitric acid	Hydrogen nitrate	-nitrate
Carbonic acid	Hydrogen carbonate	-carbonate

Alkalis

(i) **All** metal oxides are called **bases**.

Some bases dissolve in water to form **hydroxides**.

13+
C

Base	Soluble in water	Alkali formed	'Common name'
Calcium oxide	Yes	Calcium hydroxide	Lime
Copper oxide	No	–	–
Iron oxide	No	–	–
Potassium oxide	Yes	Potassium hydroxide	Caustic potash
Sodium oxide	Yes	Sodium hydroxide	Caustic soda
Zinc oxide	No	–	–

When a **base** neutralises an acid, the **first name** of the **base** becomes the **first name** of the **salt**.

$$\boxed{\textbf{acid + base}} \rightarrow \boxed{\textbf{salt + water}}$$

For example:

$$\boxed{\text{copper oxide + sulphuric acid}} \rightarrow \boxed{\text{copper sulphate + water}}$$

$$\boxed{\text{iron oxide + sulphuric acid}} \rightarrow \boxed{\text{iron sulphate + water}}$$

Carbonates can make salts

All carbonates produce carbon dioxide when added to acids – they also neutralise acids to form salts.

$$\boxed{\textbf{acid + carbonate}} \rightarrow \boxed{\textbf{salt + water + carbon dioxide}}$$

$$\boxed{\text{sulphuric acid + copper carbonate}} \rightarrow \boxed{\text{copper sulphate + water + carbon dioxide}}$$

Some metals make salts

Some metals react with acids. When they do, **salts** are formed and the gas given off is **hydrogen**.

$$\boxed{\textbf{acid + metal}} \rightarrow \boxed{\textbf{salt + hydrogen}}$$

For example:

$$\boxed{\text{sulphuric acid + zinc}} \rightarrow \boxed{\text{zinc sulphate + hydrogen}}$$

About hydrogen

- The least dense of all gases – not found in our atmosphere.

- A colourless gas that burns explosively in air to form water.

- Test with a lighted splint – a test tube of hydrogen will burn with a 'squeaky pop'.

Sample questions

Try these sample questions for yourself. The answers are given at the back of the book.

4.10 What colour will blue litmus paper go when put into the following liquids? (5)

| hydrochloric acid | limewater | sodium hydroxide | sugar solution | water |

4.11 Draw a pH scale running from 0 to 14.

On your diagram label:

(a) The neutral point. (1)

(b) Acids – showing strongest and weakest. (2)

(c) Alkalis – showing strongest and weakest. (2)

4.12 Copy out and complete the following:

(a) $\boxed{\text{Acid + base}} \rightarrow \boxed{\dots\dots\dots\dots\dots + \text{water}}$ (1)

(b) $\boxed{\text{Acid + alkali}} \rightarrow \boxed{\dots\dots\dots\dots\dots + \text{water}}$ (1)

(c) $\boxed{\text{Acid + carbonate}} \rightarrow \boxed{\dots\dots\dots\dots + \text{water} + \dots\dots\dots\dots}$ (2)

(d) $\boxed{\text{Acid + metal}} \rightarrow \boxed{\dots\dots\dots\dots + \dots\dots\dots\dots}$ (2)

(e) Adding acid to an alkali . . . . the pH of the mixture. (1)

(f) Neutralising an acid by a base . . . . the pH of the mixture. (1)

(g) Adding water to an acid . . . . the pH of the acid. (1)

4.3 A further look at oxygen

Chemical test to identify oxygen

⚠ Oxygen is the only colourless gas that re-lights a glowing splint.

Preparation of oxygen

- Thermal decomposition of potassium permanganate.

  This decomposes according to the word equation:

  | potassium permanganate (s) + heat | → | oxygen (g) + residue (s) |

  You are not expected to name the residue at this stage!

- Decomposition of hydrogen peroxide:

  | hydrogen peroxide (l) | → | oxygen (g) + water (l) |

  − This reaction is so slow that manganese oxide is added to speed up the reaction.

  − At the end of the reaction, manganese may be recovered.

  − Manganese is called a **catalyst** because it speeds up the reaction without being changed itself.

Oxygen and reactions with elements

- When magnesium burns in air, white magnesium oxide is formed.

- When copper is heated in air, there is no burning but black copper oxide is formed.

  In **both** cases, a combining reaction has taken place as each metal combines with oxygen. The combining reaction is called **oxidation**.

  − Oxidation is a chemical reaction that involves combination with oxygen.

  − When an element is oxidised, only **one** product is formed.

✓ If an exam question says '… *heated in a plentiful supply of air*', this is another way of saying **there is the opportunity of combining with oxygen**.

Oxygen and reactions with compounds

Burning a candle

When a candle burns in air, the two products **carbon dioxide** and **water** are produced. So we **know** that a candle is **not** an element, but contains at least two substances.

| candle (s) + oxygen (g) | → | water (g) + carbon dioxide (g) |

- The **hydrogen** in the water **must** have come from the candle.

- The **carbon** in the gas **must** have come from the candle.

- Looking at the word equation tells us that apart from the oxygen, **no other substances are involved**.

Candle wax is a compound that contains only **hydrogen** and **carbon**. Compounds which contain only hydrogen and carbon are called **hydrocarbons**.

| hydrocarbon + oxygen | → | energy (heat and light) + water + carbon dioxide |

Hydrocarbons are found in the many products of crude oil, e.g. petrol, candle wax, polythene and some plastics.

Oxygen and fuels

(i) **Fuels** are substances which we burn with the purpose of using the excess heat energy which is released by the reaction with oxygen.

All fuels have the following in common:

- Fuels by themselves do not release energy. It is the **fuel/oxygen reaction** which releases energy.

- Fuels contain **carbon compounds**. This means that when they burn, **carbon dioxide** is released into the atmosphere.

Types of fuels

- **Living fuels**: **wood** and materials from plants.

- **Semi-fossil fuels**: e.g. **peat**.

- **Fossil fuels**: **coal, oil, gas**. These are fuels formed from the dead remains of animals and plants that lived millions of years ago.

Burning coal

- Coal contains compounds of both carbon and sulphur.

- When coal is burnt, both gases, **carbon dioxide** and **sulphur dioxide**, are released into the atmosphere.

- Sulphur dioxide dissolves in the water of the atmosphere to form **acid rain**.

Burning gas

- Natural gas is the hydrocarbon **methane**. If your laboratory is connected to the gas supply, this is the gas which supplies your Bunsen burners.

Burning oil

● Nearly all forms of transport burn some form of hydrocarbon as a fuel.

● Hydrocarbons come from crude oil that has been separated into its various compounds by **fractional distillation** at a refinery.

● Incomplete burning of petrol causes **carbon monoxide** (a poisonous gas) to be released.

● As carbon monoxide leaves the exhaust pipe, it combines with the oxygen in the air to form carbon dioxide.

Oxygen and rusting

ⓘ The term rusting refers only to the **corrosion** of iron.

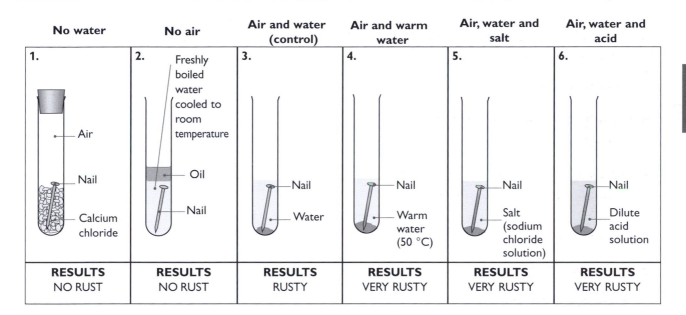

No water	No air	Air and water (control)	Air and warm water	Air, water and salt	Air, water and acid
1. Air, Nail, Calcium chloride	2. Freshly boiled water cooled to room temperature, Oil, Nail	3. Nail, Water	4. Nail, Warm water (50 °C)	5. Nail, Salt (sodium chloride solution)	6. Nail, Dilute acid solution
RESULTS NO RUST	**RESULTS** NO RUST	**RESULTS** RUSTY	**RESULTS** VERY RUSTY	**RESULTS** VERY RUSTY	**RESULTS** VERY RUSTY

● Rusting occurs when iron is exposed to **oxygen** and **water**.

● Rusting costs money (a) to replace items which have rusted, (b) to take measures to **prevent** rusting from taking place.

Three ways of preventing iron from rusting

1. **Exclude oxygen and water** by covering with a layer of **grease, oil, paint** or **plastic**.

2. **Exclude oxygen and water** by covering the iron with a **less reactive metal**, e.g. **tin**.

3. **Coat the iron with a more reactive metal**, e.g. **zinc**. This process is called **galvanising**. The zinc reacts with the water and oxygen instead of the iron, i.e. is **sacrificed** to spare the iron. This form of prevention is called **sacrificial protection**.

Sample questions

Try these sample questions for yourself. The answers are given at the back of the book.

4.13 What does the word **oxidation** mean? (2)

4.14 Methane is a hydrocarbon.

(a) What is a hydrocarbon? (1)

(b) Which two products are formed when methane burns? (2)

(c) Write a word equation to describe the burning of methane. (4)

4.15 Coal is a fossil fuel that burns well in air.

(a) What is meant by the term **fossil fuel**? (1)

(b) Name two other fossil fuels. (2)

(c) (i) Name two gases released when coal burns in air. (2)

    (ii) Suggest what happens to both of these gases when they come in contact with water vapour in the air. (2)

4.16 (a) Why is rusting said to be one of the most expensive chemical reactions? (2)

(b) Name three substances involved in rusting. (3)

(c) Describe three ways which help to prevent rusting taking place. (3)

13+
C

4.4 Comparing the reactivity of some elements

Metals are placed in order according to how well they react with oxygen, water, steam and acids in what is called the **reactivity series**.

(i) Reacting metals with oxygen

- **Sodium** and **potassium** react so well with oxygen that they have to be stored under oil. Both are soft metals and, when cut, their shiny surfaces quickly become dull as the metals react with the oxygen in the air.

- **Gold** does not react with oxygen – think of ancient Egyptian treasures that are still shiny after exposure to air (oxygen) for thousands of years.

Burning metals

Metal	Result of burning
Sodium/potassium	Reacts with oxygen without burning
Calcium	Burns with a fierce red flame
Magnesium	Burns with a brilliant white flame
Zinc	Burns with a bright, fierce blue/green flame
Iron	Burns with yellow sparks
Copper	Very hard to burn – small green flame is produced
Gold	Does not burn at all

(ii) Reacting metals with water

Metals which do so, react with water according to the word equation:

$$\boxed{\text{metal (s) + water (l)}} \rightarrow \boxed{\text{metal hydroxide (l) + hydrogen (g)}}$$

Look for:

- Bubbles of hydrogen gas.

- Formation of metal hydroxide: indicator shows alkali is present.

The following metals are added to water that has Universal Indicator added:

- **Potassium**: whizzes round; bursts into purple flame; hydrogen is given off; water changes to purple as **potassium hydroxide** is produced.

- **Sodium**: whizzes round; becomes hot enough to melt itself; hydrogen is given off; water changes to purple as **sodium hydroxide** is produced.

- **Calcium**: sinks; rapid bubbles of hydrogen appear; water changes to purple as **calcium hydroxide** is produced.

- **Magnesium**, **zinc**, **iron**, **copper**: these reactions are very slow in cold water, so reactions are speeded up by using steam.

(iii) Reacting metals with steam

$$\boxed{\text{metal (s) + steam (g)}} \rightarrow \boxed{\text{metal oxide (s) + hydrogen (g)}}$$

Look for:

- Production of the metal oxide.

- Production of hydrogen: this will burn with a yellow flame. At the end of the apparatus there is a tube which lets the gases produced, escape. The flame can be seen at the end of the tube.

Metal	Action of water	Action of steam
Potassium, sodium, calcium	React to form **metal hydroxide** and **hydrogen**	Too violent and dangerous
Magnesium, zinc, iron	Very slow reaction	React to form **metal oxide** and **hydrogen**
Copper	No reaction	No reaction

Position of hydrogen in the series

$$\boxed{\text{iron + water (hydrogen oxide)}} \rightarrow \boxed{\text{iron oxide + hydrogen}}$$

- Iron has **taken the oxygen away** from the water and has itself been **oxidised** to form iron oxide.

- The process of removal of oxygen **by another substance** is called **reduction**.

- The substance that **does the taking away** is called a **reducing agent**.

In this case, iron is the **reducing agent** which **reduces** water to hydrogen.

Look at the table above:

- Iron is able to reduce water to hydrogen – so iron is **higher** than hydrogen in the reactivity series.

- Copper is not able to reduce water – so copper is **lower** than hydrogen in the reactivity series.

(iv) Reacting metals with dilute acids

All acids are compounds of hydrogen – see section 4.1, page 78.

$$\boxed{\text{metal + acid}} \rightarrow \boxed{\text{salt + hydrogen}}$$

For example:

$$\boxed{\text{magnesium + sulphuric acid}} \rightarrow \boxed{\text{magnesium sulphate + hydrogen}}$$

So an acid is a compound containing hydrogen which can be replaced by a metal which is **higher than hydrogen** in the reactivity series.

Metal	Action of cold dilute acid	Action of warm dilute acid
Potassium, sodium	Too violent and dangerous	Too violent and dangerous
Calcium, magnesium, zinc, iron	Reacts to form salt and hydrogen	Too violent and dangerous
Tin, lead	No reaction	Reacts to form salt and hydrogen
Copper	No reaction	No reaction

Displacing metals from salts

If you put an iron nail into some copper sulphate solution, after a time:

● The solution loses its blue colour.

● The nail becomes coated with copper.

Iron, being higher than copper in the reactivity series, has **displaced copper** from copper sulphate solution.

$$\boxed{\text{iron (s) + copper sulphate (l)}} \rightarrow \boxed{\text{iron sulphate (l) + copper (s)}}$$

Metal	Reaction with magnesium chloride solution	Reaction with iron nitrate solution	Reaction with lead chloride solution	Reaction with copper sulphate solution
Magnesium	✗	✔	✔	✔
Zinc	✗	✔	✔	✔
Iron	✗	✗	✔	✔
Lead	✗	✗	✗	✔
Copper	✗	✗	✗	✗

Reacting metals with oxides

Look at part of the reactivity series:

magnesium
zinc
iron
copper

- **Magnesium** will reduce: zinc oxide, iron oxide, copper oxide.

- **Iron** will reduce **only** copper oxide.

- **Copper** could **not** reduce **any** of the oxides of iron, zinc or magnesium.

- The reaction between copper oxide and magnesium is very vigorous (products are 'blown away' in the reaction, leaving very little in the crucible).

- The reaction between copper oxide and iron is gentle (a red glow spreads through the mixture).

These results show that:

> △ **The further apart the two metals are in the reactivity series, the more violent will be the reduction reaction.**

Placing carbon in the reactivity series

Consider the following reactions you will have carried out in the laboratory:

| carbon + magnesium oxide | → | no reaction |

So magnesium is more reactive than carbon.

| carbon + zinc oxide | → | no reaction |

So zinc is more reactive than carbon, at temperatures which can be produced by a Bunsen flame (750–800 °C).

(In fact, carbon **will** reduce zinc oxide, but at a temperature of over 1000 °C.)

| carbon + iron oxide | → | iron + carbon dioxide |

So carbon is more reactive than iron (this reaction is important in the industrial production of iron).

Carbon can now be placed just **above iron**, but **below zinc** in the reactivity series.

Sample questions

Try these sample questions for yourself. The answers are given at the back of the book.

4.17 What is meant by the 'reactivity series' of metals? (1)

4.18 What do the following words mean: oxidation; reduction? (4)

4.19 Given the following order of reactivity: magnesium, zinc, iron, copper … For each of the following pairs write a word equation for any reaction that does take place.

(a) zinc + magnesium oxide (2)

(b) zinc + copper oxide (2)

(c) magnesium + iron oxide (2)

(d) iron + copper sulphate (2)

(e) iron + magnesium sulphate (2)

(f) zinc + iron sulphate (2)

4.20 You have four metals **A**, **B**, **C** and **D**. You find out that:

B reduces **C** oxide when they are heated.

There is no reaction when **B** is heated with **D** oxide.

There is no reaction when **A** is heated with **B** oxide.

Put the metals in order of reactivity (most reactive first). (4)

4.21 Copper carbonate was heated in air. It lost mass and a black powder was left as a residue.

(a) (i) What was the black powder? (1)

(ii) Write a word equation to show how the black powder can be changed to copper by heating it with carbon. (4)

(b) The black powder is added to warm dilute sulphuric acid. A blue solution is formed.

(i) What effect will the black powder have on the pH of the acid? (1)

(ii) What would you add to the solution to obtain some copper? (1)

4.22 Iron is extracted from iron oxide by heating it with carbon in a blast furnace. Write a word equation for this chemical reaction. (4)

13+
C

4.5 Metals and minerals

> ⓘ A few unreactive metals (gold, silver, copper) can be found as metals.
>
> Most metals are found as a mixture of rock and metal compound (mineral) which we call an **ore**.

Extraction of metals

- The method of extraction will depend upon the **reactivity** of the metal.

- The **higher** a metal is in the reactivity series, the **harder** it is to extract it from its ore.

Extraction of copper

- A source of copper is the mineral **malachite** (copper carbonate).

- Extraction of copper from malachite is in two stages:

  (i) Making the oxide

  | copper carbonate + heat | → | copper oxide + carbon dioxide |

  (ii) Reducing the oxide by heating with carbon

  | copper oxide + carbon | → | copper + carbon dioxide |

Extraction of iron

- The main ore is haematite (iron oxide) – a mixture of rock and iron oxide.

- Extraction is carried out in a **blast furnace** – the blast being hot air (containing oxygen).

- The raw materials (called the **charge**) which are put into the top of the furnace are:
  - Iron ore: the source of iron.
  - Limestone: to combine with the rock to form **slag**.
  - Coke: the supply of carbon.

- There are three main reactions which happen in the blast furnace:
  (i) Formation of reducing agent (carbon monoxide).
  (ii) Reduction of iron oxide.
  (iii) Formation of slag.

(i) Formation of the reducing agent

1. Coke burns in the hot blast to form carbon dioxide.

   | carbon + oxygen | → | carbon dioxide |

2. Limestone (calcium carbonate) decomposes to release carbon dioxide.

   | calcium carbonate + heat | → | calcium oxide + carbon dioxide |

3. Carbon dioxide passes over more hot coke to form carbon monoxide.

   | carbon dioxide + carbon | → | carbon monoxide |

(ii) Reduction of iron oxide

Carbon monoxide reduces iron oxide and the iron formed is molten at the high temperature (1800 °C) produced, and runs to the bottom of the furnace where it collects until it is **tapped** (run off).

iron oxide + carbon monoxide	→	iron + carbon dioxide

(iii) Formation of slag

The 'rocky' part of the iron ore will be mainly composed of sandy substances such as silicon oxide. This will combine with the calcium oxide (from stage 1(ii)), to form slag. Slag will be molten and so drips to the bottom of the furnace where it floats on the more dense iron.

sandy rock (silicon oxide) + calcium oxide	→	slag (calcium silicate)

Extraction of aluminium

- Aluminium is higher than iron in the reactivity series and cannot be reduced by heating with carbon.

- Extraction requires a large supply of electricity and high temperatures.

- The main mineral source is **bauxite** (aluminium oxide).

- Bauxite is purified chemically and is dissolved in molten **cryolite**. The cryolite lowers the temperature at which the ore melts (otherwise the furnace temperature would need to be over 2000 °C) and the solution has an electric current passed through it to extract the aluminium metal.

Limestone

- Calcium carbonate is the main compound in limestone.

- Limestone is a sedimentary rock made by the decomposition of the shells of creatures that lived in the ancient seas.

Uses of limestone

Building	Used as 'bricks' for houses. Although they look good, they are prone to attack from acid rain over the years
Extraction of iron	One of the ingredients of a blast furnace
Manufacture of cement	The basic ingredient in two important substances used in the construction industry: **mortar** (the 'glue' that binds bricks together) and **cement** (an important part of concrete)
Manufacture of lime	An alkali that is used by farmers and growers to neutralise acid soils

Sample questions

Try these sample questions for yourself. The answers are given at the back of the book.

4.23 Bronze is an alloy (mixture) of copper and tin. Explain why knowledge of chemistry will help you to remember that the Bronze Age came before the Iron Age. (3)

4.24 Iron is higher in the reactivity series than lead. The main ore of lead is galena (lead sulphide) and lead oxide is reduced by carbon.

(a) Write a word equation to show how you change galena into lead oxide. (5)

(b) Write a word equation for the reduction of lead oxide. (5)

(c) Would iron reduce lead oxide? Give a reason. (2)

4.25 Iron is made in a blast furnace. Materials loaded into the furnace are called the charge. Molten liquids are 'tapped' from the bottom of the furnace.

(a) Why is the furnace called a blast furnace and what is the purpose of the blast? (2)

(b) Which materials form the charge and what is the purpose of each material? (6)

(c) What is the main reducing agent? (1)

(d) Write a word equation for the main reduction in the furnace. (4)

(e) Which two liquids are 'tapped' at the bottom of the furnace? (2)

4.26 Below is a table which tells you about the extraction of three metals.

Metal	Extraction
Aluminium	From aluminium oxide by a chemical reaction involving large amounts of electricity
Gold	By crushing the ore and washing it
Iron	From iron oxide by a chemical reaction with carbon

(a) Put the three metals in order of increasing reactivity. (3)

(b) Aluminium is more expensive than iron even though it is more abundant. Why is this? (2)

(c) Why is gold much more expensive than aluminium? (2)

Summary

You should now know the following:

1.   How substances can be classified and how they can change state.

2.   The differences between pure and impure substances.

3.   The main features of the Periodic Table.

4.   How to separate mixtures.

5.   How indicators are used to identify particular substances.

6.   The main features of salts.

7.   The main features of oxygen and how it reacts with different elements and compounds.

8.   How metals react with different substances.

9.   The main features of unreactive metals and minerals.

Use the glossary at the back of the book for definitions of key words.

13+

C

Test yourself

Before moving on to the next chapter, make sure you can answer the following questions. The answers are at the back of the book.

1.   (a) What is an element?

       (b) Approximately, how many elements are there?

       (c) Where can you find a list of all known elements?

       (d) What is significant about the atoms of elements?

2.   What are, and where can you find:

       (a) Electrons?

       (b) Neutrons?

       (c) Protons?

3.   List two important features of **all** chemical reactions.

4.   (a) What does an indicator do?

       (b) Name four indicators and say what they are used for.

5.   Which of the following will turn red litmus blue?

       (a) Hydrochloric acid.

       (b) Limewater.

       (c) Sodium hydroxide.

       (d) Sugar solution.

       (e) Water.

6. How would you test a gas to show that it is oxygen?

7. Write word equations that describe what happens when the following burn in a plentiful supply of air:

   (a) Carbon.

   (b) Magnesium.

   (c) Sulphur.

8. Write a word equation for each of the reactions described below.

   (a) An iron nail becomes pink if placed in copper sulphate solution.

   (b) Copper foil becomes pale grey if placed in silver nitrate solution.

9. What is an ore?

10. Aluminium, copper, glass, iron lead, plastic, rubber. From this list, choose one that would be the most suitable for the uses given below. In each case, give a reason for your choice.

    (a) A picnic mug.

    (b) The inner wires of an electric cable.

    (c) The guttering round the roof of a house.

    (d) A bucket to carry red hot ashes.

    (e) Wings of an aeroplane.

PHYSICS

Chapter 5: 11+ Physics

5.1 Electric circuits

- Lamps, motors and buzzers work when an electric current passes through them.

- Electric current moves **from the +** (positive) terminal through the circuit **to the –** (negative) terminal of a cell/battery.

- A **battery** is made up of two or more cells connected together.

- Electric current moves through wires (leads) which are **electrical conductors**.

> For an electric circuit to work:
>
> - There **must be no gaps**, i.e. there must be a complete circuit.
> - **All cells must face the same way**, i.e. be the same way round.

Drawing electric circuits

- Circuits should be drawn as **straight lines** for the conducting wires.

- **Circuit symbols** should be drawn to represent the various components (lamps, cells, etc.).

Circuit symbols

COMPONENT	SYMBOL	WHAT THE COMPONENT IS USED FOR
Cell (battery)	—|⊢—	Provides electrical energy for the circuit.
Power supply (Lab Pack)	—o o—	Alternative to using cells.
Wire (lead)	———	Lets electric current travel through it.
Bulb/lamp	—⊗—	Converts electrical energy into heat and light energy.
Motor	—(M)—	Converts electrical energy into movement energy.
Buzzer	—⊲	Converts electrical energy into sound energy.
Push-button switch	—o▪o—	When pressed, it completes the circuit, allowing the current to flow.
Switch	—╱o—	When closed, it completes the circuit, allowing the current to flow.

Adding cells or lamps

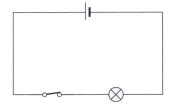

- The lamp, cell and switch are connected **in series** – the components are connected one after another.

- The lamp is said to shine with '**normal brightness**'.

- **Adding more lamps** makes each lamp **dimmer**.

- **Adding another cell** makes the lamp in the circuit **brighter**.

In general:

⚠ If the number of **cells** = the number of **lamps**, the lamps are of **normal brightness**.

If the number of **cells** > the number of **lamps**, the lamps are **brighter** than normal brightness.

If the number of **cells** < the number of **lamps**, the lamps are **dimmer** than normal brightness.

The misnamed 'short circuit'

- This is misnamed because it has **nothing to do with length**.

- Electric current will **always** take the **easiest route**.

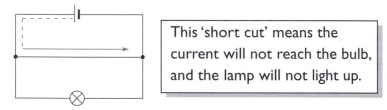

This 'short cut' means the current will not reach the bulb, and the lamp will not light up.

A fault in mains equipment could cause a person to receive an electric shock. To prevent this, an **earth** wire is found in most plugs. The earth wire is the short circuit that takes the current to the ground rather than passing through a person.

Sample questions

Try these sample questions for yourself. The answers are given at the back of the book.

5.1 Copy out and complete the sentences below using the following words:

| bright normal brightness dim |

(a) If the number of cells = the number of lamps, the lamps are .... (1)

(b) If the number of cells > the number of lamps, the lamps are .... (1)

(c) If the number of cells < the number of lamps, the lamps are .... (1)

5.2 (a) Draw a circuit with two cells in series with three lamps and a switch. (3)

(b) What will be the brightness of the lamps? (1)

(c) Give three possible reasons (apart from 'the battery is flat') why the lamps do not light when the switch is closed. (3)

5.3 Why can the term **short circuit** be rather misleading? (2)

5.2 Forces and motion

What is a force?

- A force is an **invisible push** or **pull** – you can only see what a force does.

- A force can:
  - Make a stationary object **move**.
  - Make a moving object go **faster** or **slower**.
  - Make a moving object **change direction**.
  - Make a moving object **stop**.
  - **Change** the **shape** of an object.

ⓘ **Key facts about forces**

- **All forces** (i) have **size**; (ii) **act in one direction only**.
  - We measure the **size** of a force in **newtons (N)** using a **newton meter** (newton spring balance).

- We show the **direction** and **size** of a force by drawing **arrows**:

  large arrow – large force

  small arrow – small force

- **Forces act in pairs in opposite directions**.
  - When the forces are **equal**, the forces are **balanced** – **no movement** happens.
  - If one force is **bigger** than the other, the forces are **unbalanced** – **movement** happens **in the same direction as the larger force acts**.

- When a force acts, the other force of the pair acting in the opposite direction is called the **reaction force**.

11+

P

Types of force

Magnetic forces

- A freely suspended magnet will **always** have the **same end** pointing towards the geographical North Pole, so this end is called the **north-seeking pole**. The other end is called the **south-seeking pole**.

- A **compass needle** is a small magnet.

- **Only** materials containing **iron** (e.g. steel) will be attracted by a magnet – such materials are called **magnetic**.

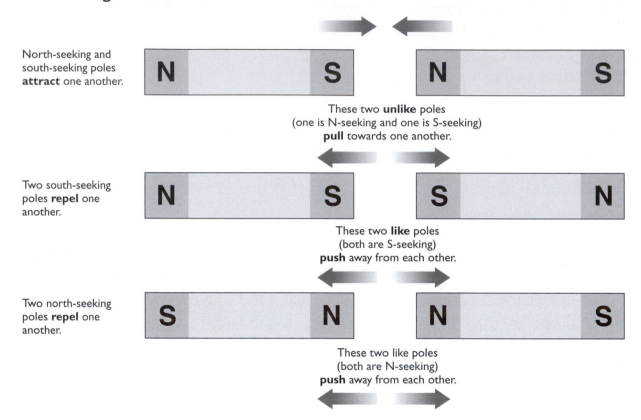

North-seeking and south-seeking poles **attract** one another.

These two **unlike** poles (one is N-seeking and one is S-seeking) **pull** towards one another.

Two south-seeking poles **repel** one another.

These two **like** poles (both are S-seeking) **push** away from each other.

Two north-seeking poles **repel** one another.

These two like poles (both are N-seeking) **push** away from each other.

Gravitational force

- Gravity is the force of attraction between **any** masses.

- Gravity **never pushes** – it only **pulls**.

- The **size** of gravitational force depends upon:
  - The mass of the object.
  - The distance between the centre of each object.

- Gravity pulls all objects towards the centre of the Earth. So all objects will exert a downwards force which is called the object's **weight**.

- **Weight is measured in newtons (N)** using a newton meter.

Floating and sinking

- Water exerts an upward force (**upthrust**) on all objects.

- Gravity exerts a downward force (**weight**) on all objects.

- When these two forces are **balanced** (equal), the object **floats**.

- If **weight > upthrust** the object **sinks**.

Friction

- Friction occurs when **any** two surfaces rub together. Even the smoothest surfaces have ridges and high spots when looked at through a microscope.

- The high spots will try to stick together and the ridges oppose movement.

ⓘ Friction is the force which opposes motion.

- Aeroplanes moving through the air will rub against air particles that will slow down the movement in a special type of friction called **air resistance**.

ⓘ **A parachute jump**

When the parachutist leaves the aeroplane:

weight > air resistance – parachutist speeds up as he/she falls (unbalanced forces).

When the parachute has opened:

weight = air resistance – parachutist falls at a steady speed (balanced forces).

Friction in action

- Rough road surfaces and tyres with patterned ridges (tread) enable cars and cycles to (i) move; (ii) be easier to control.

- Carpets are safer to walk on than polished, shiny floors.

- Brake pads are designed to produce as **large** a frictional force as possible, to slow down or stop a moving vehicle.

- Cars, aeroplanes and cycle helmets are specially shaped (**streamlined**) to reduce the friction with air particles during movement.

- Friction may be reduced by putting a layer of oil (**lubrication**) to keep the rough surfaces apart.

Sample questions

Try these sample questions for yourself. The answers are given at the back of the book.

5.4 List **four** things that force can do. (4)

5.5 Suggest which forces are balanced when a boat floats. (2)

5.6 What is meant by a **reaction force**. (1)

5.7 Copy out and complete the following sentences.

(a) Materials that are attracted by a magnet are said to be . . . . (1)

(b) The end of a magnet that points towards the geographical north pole
is called the . . . . (1)

(c) . . . . poles attract; . . . . poles repel. (2)

5.8 (a) What is the name of the force that gravity exerts on all objects on Earth? (1)

(b) What is the direction of this force? (1)

5.9 (a) What is friction? (1)

(b) When does friction take place? (1)

5.10 List **four** parts of a bicycle where friction is evident. In each case, suggest if friction
is a help or a nuisance. (8)

5.3 Light and sound

Light

We see objects because light energy activates receptors found in our eyes. The light energy entering our eyes comes from one of two sources:

- **Luminous source**: the Sun, a lamp, the stars, a television set give out their own light.

- **Reflection from non-luminous objects**: these do **not** give out light, but we see them because light from a luminous source is **reflected into** our eyes.

How we see things

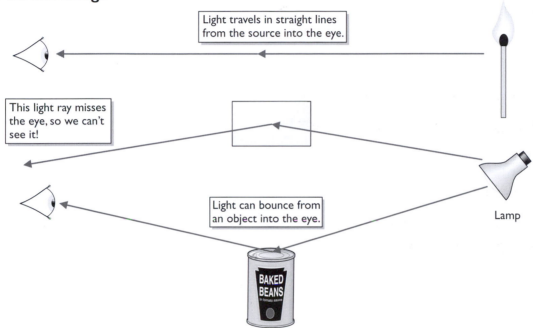

Light travels in straight lines from the source into the eye.

This light ray misses the eye, so we can't see it!

Light can bounce from an object into the eye.

Lamp

How light travels

- **Light travels very fast** – nothing yet has been found to travel faster.

- **Light rays travel in straight lines** – you cannot see round corners.

- **Light rays travel through some materials:**

  - **Transparent materials**, e.g. **glass**, **water**. Light rays will pass through these materials and you **can** see clear images through them.

  - **Translucent materials**, e.g. **tracing paper**, **some plastics**. Some light rays are changed as they pass through these materials, which means that you **cannot** see a clear image of what is on the other side.

  - **Opaque materials**, e.g. **wood**, **metal**, **pottery**. Light rays **cannot pass through** these materials at all. Such materials block light rays and form **shadows**.

Looking at shadows

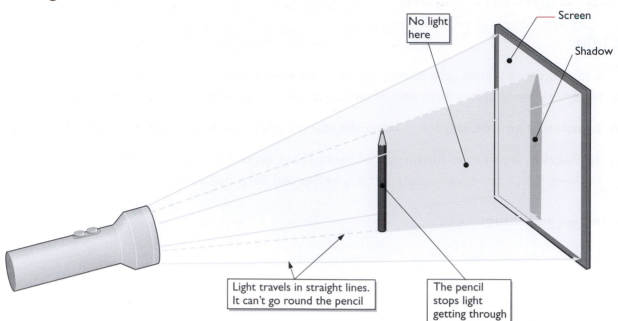

No light here

Screen

Shadow

Light travels in straight lines. It can't go round the pencil

The pencil stops light getting through

- To make the shadow **larger**: (i) move the pencil closer to the light source, or (ii) move the screen further away from the pencil.

- To make the shadow **smaller**: (i) move the pencil away from the light source, or (ii) move the screen closer to the pencil.

- The sharp outlines of the shadow of the pencil confirms that light travels in straight lines.

Reflection of light

- **Shiny surfaces**, e.g. mirrors, bounce light rays off the surface **at the same angle** as they hit the mirror surface. This is called **reflection**.

- **Rough surfaces**, e.g. paper, stone, cloth, reflect light rays in many directions – the light has been **scattered**.

Sound

- When a guitar string is plucked, it moves backwards and forwards, i.e. **it vibrates**.

- Each vibration causes the surrounding air to be squashed and stretched in pulses and so **sound waves** are formed.

- **Vibrations cause sound waves to be produced**.

- When sound waves meet our ear drum, similar vibrations are set up in our ear. These vibrations are changed into messages in the ear which are sent to the brain, so we hear the sound of the guitar string.

- Sound waves need something to stretch and squash, so they are able to travel through **solids** and **liquids** as well as air and other gases.

ⓘ There are **no** particles at all in a **vacuum** (nothing to squash and stretch), so **sound cannot travel through a vacuum**.

Loudness

● This depends upon the **energy of the vibration**, i.e. how **hard** something is plucked or hit.

● **More energy used in the hitting/plucking** results in **larger vibrations** which produce **louder sounds**.

Pitch

● Pitch describes how **high** or **low** a sound is.

● Pitch is determined by the:

– **Length** of vibrating material. **Shortening** a vibrating string **increases** the pitch of a sound. Shortening the string makes the vibrations faster. **Faster vibrations** result in **higher pitched** sounds.

– **Amount** of vibrating material. **Increasing** the amount (thickness) of a string, **lowers** the pitch of a sound. Heavier (thicker) strings have more mass to move, so vibrate more slowly. **Slower vibrations** result in **lower pitched sounds**.

Sample questions

Try these sample questions for yourself. The answers are given at the back of the book.

5.11 A table is a non-luminous source and yet we can see it. Explain how this is possible.   (2)

5.12 Write down the words which complete the following sentences:

(a) Light rays will pass through . . . . materials and you can see clear images through them.   (1)

(b) Light rays cannot pass through . . . . materials at all. Such materials block light rays and form shadows.   (1)

(c) Some light rays are changed as they pass through . . . . materials, which means that you cannot see a clear image of what is on the other side.   (1)

5.13 What happens when a light ray hits a mirror and what is this called?   (2)

5.14 How are sound waves produced?   (2)

5.15 (a) Describe how you would make a guitar string produce a musical note.   (2)

(b) How would you make the note higher?   (2)

(c) How would you make the sound louder?   (1)

5.16 Why can we not hear the vast explosions which constantly take place on the Sun? ('The huge distance' is not the answer!)   (2)

5.4 The Earth and the solar system

The solar system

- The nearest star to the Earth is the Sun.

- The Earth, together with the other main planets, orbit the Sun making what is known as the **solar system**.

- The Earth, Sun and all the planets are approximately spherical in shape.

- A planet is a body that **orbits a star**.

- The Earth takes **365¼** days to orbit the Sun – this is called a **year**.

- The Earth spins on its own axis and makes one complete turn every 24 hours – this is called one **day**.

✓ To help you remember the order of the planets, use the phrase:

My Very Eccentric Mother Just Shot Uncle Norman's Pig.

- The Earth is one of eight main planets and the dwarf planet Pluto that orbit the Sun.

- As the Earth spins:
  - Half of it is lit up by the Sun – **daytime**.
  - The other half is in darkness – **night-time**.

The Sun and the Earth

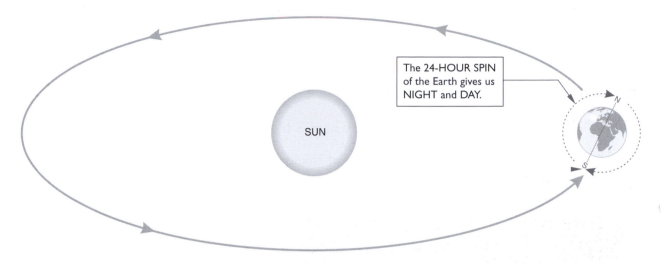

The 24-HOUR SPIN of the Earth gives us NIGHT and DAY.

SUN

Sunshine and shadows

- The Sun appears to rise in the east, become high at midday and appears to set in the west. In fact, the Sun **does not move**, **it is the spinning of the Earth** that causes this.

- Opaque objects that block out sunlight cause **shadows**. These vary in **length** and **direction** throughout the day:

Time of day	Position of sun	Shadow
Morning	Sun is low in the sky	Shadows are long and point west.
Midday	Sun is high in the sky	Shadows are shortest and point north.
Evening	Sun is low in the sky	Shadows are long and point east.

- The changing length and direction of shadows is used in the design of **sundials** which are used to tell the time of day.

The Moon

- A moon is a body which **orbits a planet**.

- The general name given to a body that orbits a planet is a **satellite**.

- Each of the planets, except Mercury and Venus, has at least one satellite (called a moon) that orbits them.

- The Earth has **one** satellite (the **Moon**) and this orbits the Earth once every 28 days. This period of time is called one **lunar month**.

- **The Moon is not a light source** and it is hard to see during daytime. We see it best at night because light from the Sun is reflected from it.

- We do not always see the whole Moon all the time: it appears to change shape at different times of the month. We call these changes in the shape of the Moon **phases**.

Sample questions

Try these sample questions for yourself. The answers are given at the back of the book.

5.17 Why do we experience night and day?   (1)

5.18 What causes the Sun to appear to move across the sky?   (1)

5.19 Explain the difference in the appearance of shadows cast at midday and in the evening.   (2)

5.20 How long is a lunar month and what does this period of time represent?   (2)

5.21 Why can we see the Moon better at night than in the daytime?   (2)

Summary

You should now know the following:

1.   The basic elements of an electric circuit.

2.   How to draw electric circuits and circuit symbols.

3.   The effect of adding different elements to circuits.

4.   The main types and features of forces.

5.   The main features of light.

6.   The main features of sound.

7.   The main features of the solar system.

Use the glossary at the back of the book for definitions of key words.

Test yourself

Before moving on to the next chapter, make sure you can answer the following questions. The answers are at the back of the book.

1. Draw and label the following circuit symbols:

    (a) A lamp.

    (b) A cell.

    (c) A switch.

    (d) A motor.

2. If lamps and cells are connected **in series**, what does this mean?

3. What is a force?

4. What do we measure force in?

5. What do we use to measure force?

6. What is gravity?

7. What does gravity **never** do?

8. Give three examples of luminous sources.

9. Name two important features which describe how light travels.

10. (a) How long does it take for the Earth to complete one orbit of the Sun?

    (b) What do we call this period of time?

11. What is the difference between a moon and a planet?

11+

P

Chapter 6: 13+ Physics

6.1 Mass, volume and density

Mass

- The mass tells us **how much matter** is present.

- The **standard unit** of mass is the **kilogram (kg)**, but you will normally measure mass in **grams (g)**.

- There is no verb 'to mass', so we call the activity **weighing**. Objects are weighed on balances (or scales) and the mass is read off the scale in kilograms or grams.

> (i) **Do not confuse mass and weight**.
>
> **Mass** is the **amount of material** in a body – measured in kilograms (or grams).
>
> **Weight** is the **downward force** exerted by a body because of gravity – measured in newtons (N).

Volume

- Volume tells us **how big** a solid object is. In the case of a liquid, it tells us **how much liquid** we have.

- In the laboratory, it is usual to measure volume in **cubic centimetres (cm^3)**.

Measuring liquids

It is usual to measure the volume of liquids by using a **measuring cylinder**. Some measuring cylinders are marked in litres (l) or millilitres (ml). As 1 litre of water has almost the same volume as 1000 cm^3, it is perfectly satisfactory to measure liquids in cm^3.

Measuring the volume of solids

(i) Regular shaped solids

Simply measure the length (l), width (w) and height (h) and multiply them together.

> **volume = l x w x h cm^3**

(ii) Irregular shaped solids

A non-porous solid will push away (displace) water.

> **volume of object = amount of water displaced**

(a) Using a measuring cylinder

Put some water in a measuring cylinder – **old volume**.

↓

Submerge the object in the water, which rises – **new volume**.

↓

volume of object = new volume – old volume

(b) Using a displacement ('Eureka') can

Fill the can with water until water comes out of the spout.

↓

Wait for the water to stop dripping out of the spout.

↓

Place an empty measuring cylinder under the spout.

↓

Submerge the object in the can and read off the volume of water collected in the measuring cylinder.

↓

volume of object = volume of water in the measuring cylinder

Measuring the volume of gases

Gases fill any container completely, so we measure the **size of the container**. This could be a measuring cylinder (inverted over water) or, more usually, a **gas syringe**.

Density

- Each and every substance has its own special number called its **density**, which describes how much matter (**mass**) is packed into a **specified volume** (usually 1 cm³) of it.

- Density can be used to **identify** a substance.

- The **density** of a material is the **mass** of **each** cm³.

- The unit of density is **g/cm³**.

13+

P

Density of solids

Find the **mass** of the object.

↓

Find the **volume** of the object.

↓

Calculate using the relationship:

↓

density = mass/volume

Density of liquids

Weigh an empty measuring cylinder – call it **C** g.

↓

Take the measuring cylinder **off the scales** and pour in the liquid.

↓

Weigh the measuring cylinder + liquid – call it (**C + L**) g.

↓

Mass of liquid = (C + L) – C g = L g.

↓

Read off the **volume** of liquid in the cylinder.

↓

Use **D = M/V** to calculate density.

Density of gases

(i) Density of oxygen

Potassium permanganate decomposes when it is heated to form a solid residue and releases oxygen as described by the word equation:

$$\boxed{\text{potassium permanganate (s) + heat}} \rightarrow \boxed{\text{residue (s) + oxygen (g)}}$$

As **total mass at start = total mass at end**, then:

mass of oxygen = (mass of potassium permanganate) − (mass of residue)

The **volume** of oxygen is found by collecting the gas in a gas syringe.

(ii) Density of carbon dioxide

A similar experiment using the **same** apparatus can be carried out, this time by heating a suitable carbonate, e.g. copper carbonate instead of potassium permanganate. The experimental procedure is exactly the same; it is the **reaction** that is different:

$$\boxed{\text{copper carbonate (s) + heat}} \rightarrow \boxed{\text{copper oxide (s) + carbon dioxide (g)}}$$

Sample questions

Try these sample questions for yourself. The answers are given at the back of the book.

6.1   Which **two** things do you need to know about a substance to be able to find out its density? (2)

6.2   Using the words **density**, **mass** and **volume**, write down the equation which you would use to find density. (3)

6.3   Find the densities of the following blocks of materials:

   (a) Material **A**, mass 750 g, volume 100 cm^3. (2)

   (b) Material **B**, mass 220 g, volume 20 cm^3. (2)

   (c) Material **C**, mass 540 g, volume 200 cm^3. (2)

   (d) Material **D**, mass 162 g, volume 60 cm^3. (2)

6.4   In question 6.3, which of the blocks **A, B, C, D** are made of the **same** material? Give a reason. (2)

6.5   The density of marble is 3.2 g/cm^3; the density of glass is 2.8 g/cm^3. If you had 3 kg of each, which material would have the larger volume? (1)

6.6   If the density of air is 1.3×10^{-3} g/cm^3, what is the mass of air in a room measuring 10 m x 6 m x 3 m? (2)

6.2 Electricity and magnetism

Electricity

- When one end of a conductor has a greater amount of energy than the other, **electric charge** in the form of electrons will flow in the form of an **electric current**.

- The energy difference, sometimes called **potential** (energy) **difference** or **p.d.**, is measured in **volts (V)**.

- The **amount of current** is measured in **amperes** or **amps (A)** using an **ammeter** that needs to be connected **in series**.

- Ammeters **must be connected the right way – positive (on ammeter) to positive (on battery/cell)**.

- A battery is made up of two or more cells connected together. A cell or battery transforms chemical energy into electrical energy, and this electrical energy is changed into other forms in electric components.

Electric circuits

(i) Series circuits

- **One path** for the current to travel.

- Components are connected one after the other.

- Current is **not** used up as it goes round a series circuit. This means that current is the same at all points in a series circuit.

- Adding more **cells**, increases the available energy (more volts).

- Adding more **components** (e.g. lamps, motors), puts more 'things in the way' (increases resistance to the current) so current becomes less.

(ii) Parallel circuits

- **Two/more** individual circuits, each one being connected to the **same** power supply.

- Each component draws its **own** supply of current from the cell/battery.

- Adding extra components means **more current** is drawn so the battery/cell **runs down more quickly**.

- If **one** component fails, components in **other circuits** are **not affected**.

Current in a parallel circuit

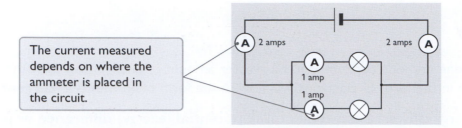

The current measured depends on where the ammeter is placed in the circuit.

Resistance

- **Increasing resistance decreases** the amount of **current** in a circuit.

- **Resistors transform energy** (also known as the **heating effect** of a current).

- **Good conductors** (e.g. copper, gold) offer **low resistance** to current.

- **Thick** wire offers **less resistance** to current than **thin** wire.

Resistors: components designed to reduce current

- **Fixed value**

resistor

The amount of resistance can be measured and is recorded in **Ohms (Ω)**.

- **Variable**

Symbols for a variable resistor

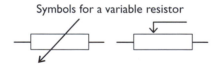

These are sometimes called '**dimmers**'.

- **LDR (light-dependent resistor)**

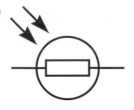

light-dependent resistor

✓ Think of **L, L, L**.

'An **L**DR has **L**ow resistance in **L**ight.'

When light falls on an LDR, the value of its resistance falls. **In the dark**, an LDR has **high resistance**.

- **Fuse**

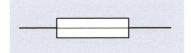

Used as a safety device to protect components from damage caused by high currents.

> ### ⓘ **How a fuse works**
>
> When there is a current in a circuit which is too high for the fuse, the fuse wire **heats – melts – and breaks** the circuit, stopping all current in the circuit immediately.

Switches

Their function is to complete or break circuits.

Switch closed: 'ON' – circuit complete; current flows.

Switch open: 'OFF' – circuit broken; no current flows.

Types of switches

1. **'Normal' toggle switch**, e.g. light switch.

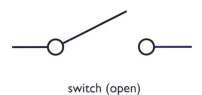

switch (open)

2. **Push switch**, e.g. bell push, mobile phone and computer keys.

push-button switch

3. **Reed switch**: Contacts normally open – needs a magnet to close them.

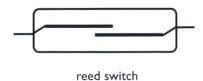

reed switch

Combining switches

(i) Switches in series: a simple 'AND' circuit

- Used for safety devices in machines, e.g. safety screens, washing machine doors.

- The motor **works** only when switches A **AND** B are closed.

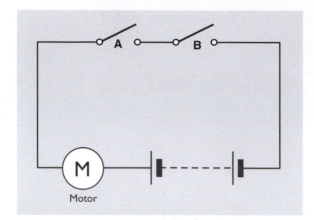

AND circuit: Both switch A **AND** switch B must be on before the motor will run.

- Results can be summarised in a **truth table**.

- The **input** being provided by switches A and B.

- The **output**, in this case, is the motor.

Inputs		Output
Switch A	**Switch B**	**Motor**
Off	Off	Off
Off	On	Off
On	Off	Off
On	On	On

- Switch ON: current flows – represented by **1**.

- Switch OFF: no current – represented by **0**.

- **Output** is represented by **Q**.

Inputs		Output
A	**B**	**Q**
0	0	0
0	1	0
1	0	0
1	1	1

(ii) Switches in parallel: a simple 'OR' circuit

- Used for burglar alarms, car interior lights.

- The bell **sounds** when switches A **OR** B, **OR BOTH**, are closed.

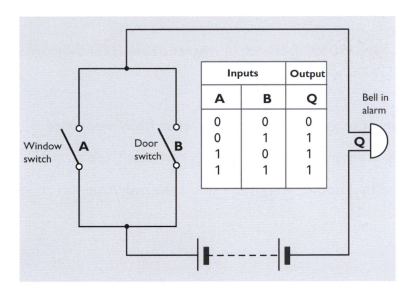

Inputs		Output
A	**B**	**Q**
0	0	0
0	1	1
1	0	1
1	1	1

OR circuit: If either switch A or switch B is on the alarm will sound.

Diodes

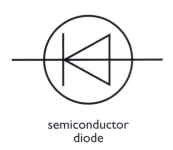

semiconductor
diode

- Made from materials called **semiconductors** which allow current to flow through them one way, but almost no current to flow through the other.

- Used to protect components that would be damaged if current flowed through them the wrong way, e.g. in radios and computers.

- Their purpose is to allow current to flow in **one direction only**.

- Current flows in the **same direction in which the arrow on the symbol points**.

Light-emitting diode (LED)

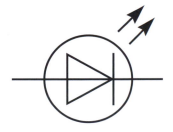

light-emitting diode

- Diode that **emits light** when a small **current flows** through it.

- A protective resistor is always connected in series with an LED to protect it from damage caused by too large a current flowing through it.

- **Must** be connected the right way: **positive → anode; negative → cathode**.

Magnetism

See Chapter 5, Section 5.2, page 110 for details of: (i) magnetic poles; (ii) how magnets behave.

Testing magnets

- Magnets will settle and point to **geographical north** when freely suspended.

- Magnets will attract **only** other magnetic materials, e.g. iron (steel), cobalt, nickel.

- Magnets will be **repulsed by another magnet** – this is the **only** true test to identify a magnet.

Magnetic field

- The area around a magnet where a magnetic force can be detected.

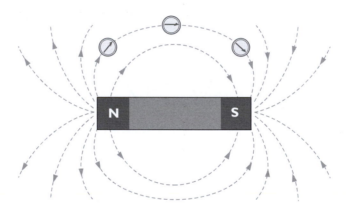

- The lines are called **lines of force**.

- The **arrows** show the direction in which the force acts.

> ✓ The direction of the force can be remembered by the word
> '**NAST**': **N**orth **A**way – **S**outh **T**owards

- The **spacing** of the lines tells us the **strength** of the field:
  - Lines closer together is **stronger** than lines further apart.

- The lines are **invisible** – we only see them because of the use of iron filings.

Using electricity to make magnets – the magnetic effect of an electric current

Making an electromagnet

- When a current flows through a wire, a magnetic field exists around the wire.

- A compass needle shows that this magnetic field will have direction.

- If the direction of the current is changed, the needle points in the opposite direction.

- If the wire is formed into a loop, the magnetic field will be in one direction, **at right angles to the loop**. Reversing the direction of the current will reverse the direction of the magnetic field.

- If more loops are added using **insulated** wire, as in a **coil**, there is a strong magnetic field **inside** the coil which:

    – Ceases if the current stops flowing.

    – Is in one particular direction.

    – Will reverse in direction if the direction of the current is reversed.

- A soft iron rod (**core**) placed inside the coil will become a magnet when the current is switched on.

> **To make an electromagnet stronger:**
>
> - Add more turns of insulated wire to the coil.
>
> - Increase the current.
>
> - Add a 'core' of soft iron.

Using an electromagnet

- **Metal scrapyards**

    – Iron and steel can be separated from non-magnetic materials.

    – Iron can be lifted, moved and dropped where it is needed when the current is switched off.

- **Relays**

    A relay is a switch which is operated by an electromagnet and consists of **two separate circuits**:

    – **Circuit 1**: the ON/OFF switch controls a **small** current which is used to make the coil a magnet.

    – **Circuit 2**: the 'end use' circuit (e.g. car starter motor) – currents in these circuits can be quite large.

Sample questions

Try these sample questions for yourself. The answers are given at the back of the book.

6.7 (a) Draw a circuit which contains two cells, a lamp and an ammeter in series. (4)

(b) What happens to the ammeter reading if another lamp is added to the circuit? (1)

(c) What must you be careful about when connecting the ammeter? (1)

6.8 Look at the circuit below:

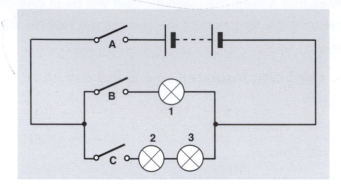

(a) Which switch (i) controls all lamps; (ii) controls lamp 1? (2)

(b) Which switches would you close to light (i) lamp 1; (ii) lamps 2 and 3? (2)

6.9 James set up a circuit containing two cells, two lamps and two fuses in series. James thought that a fuse was needed for each lamp.

(a) Is James correct? Give a reason for your answer. (2)

(b) Describe how a fuse works. (2)

(c) What is the purpose of a fuse? (2)

6.10 (a) How would you use a cell and some insulated wire to magnetise an iron nail? (3)

(b) How would you test the iron nail to show that it had become a magnet? (2)

(c) What could you do to make the nail a stronger magnet? (2)

6.11 A table lamp (**Q**) has a switch on it (**A**). The lamp is plugged into the mains supply at a socket which has a switch (**B**).

(a) What type of circuit is this? (1)

(b) Draw a truth table for the circuit (use 0, 1). (9)

6.3 Forces and motion

See also Chapter 5, Section 5.2, page 109 for:

- **What a force is**.
- **What a force can do**.

Speed

- This is a measure of **how fast** something is moving.
- We need to measure:
  - The distance the object moves (**m**).
  - The **time** it takes to move this distance (**s**).
- Speed is the distance moved in **each second**. This gives us the unit of speed as **m/s**.
- To calculate speed:

speed = distance/time (or S = D/T)

Weight

ⓘ **All masses will be pulled towards the Earth's centre by gravitational force (g)**.

On Earth, gravity pulls each kg of mass with a force of about 10 N, i.e. we say **g ≈ 10 N/kg** (≈ means 'approximately equal to').

This is confirmed by the use of a newton spring balance (or **newton meter**).

Mass	Weight (reading on newton meter)
1 kg	10 N
2 kg	20 N
0.5 kg	5 N

From these results, we can see that:

weight (N) = mass (kg) × gravitational force (N/kg)

ⓘ **Mass stays the same; weight changes from planet to planet.**

Travels of a 5 kg mass

Earth	Earth's Moon	Outer space
mass = 5 kg	mass = 5 kg	mass = 5 kg
g = 10 N/kg	g = 1.6 N/kg	g = 0
weight =5 kg × 10 N/kg	weight = 5 kg × 1.6 N/kg	weight = 5 kg × 0 N/kg
= 50 N	= 8 N	= 0*

* This is why masses become **weightless** in space.

131

Balanced forces

ⓘ **Forces act in pairs in opposite directions**.

When the forces are **equal**, the forces are **balanced** – **no movement** happens.

If one force is **bigger** than the other, the forces are **unbalanced** – **movement** happens **in the direction in which the larger force acts**.

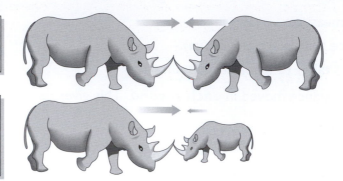

Balanced (equal) forces: No movement

Unbalanced (unequal) forces: Smaller object moves to the right

Stationary objects

- The **downward force** exerted by the weight of a book at rest on a table, is **balanced** by the **upward force** exerted by the table.

- A boat floats because the **downward force** exerted by the weight of the boat is **balanced** by the upward force (**upthrust**) exerted by the water.

Moving objects

- If a force acts on a moving body **in the same direction** as the movement, the body will **increase** in speed (i.e. **accelerate**).

  For example:

  – Gravity increases the speed of falling objects.

  – Pedalling harder makes your bicycle go faster.

- If a force acts on a moving body **in the opposite direction** to the movement, then the body will **decrease** in speed (i.e. slow down).

- When the two opposing forces are **equal** (i.e. **are balanced**), the body will **move at a constant speed**.

- When the two opposing forces are **not equal** (i.e. **are unbalanced**), the body will **change speed and/or direction**.

Friction – the force that opposes motion

- Objects moving through the air will rub against air particles which slow them down. This is a form of friction called **air resistance** (**drag**).

- To **reduce** the effect of air resistance, bodies are given pointed fronts, sleek designs and smooth surfaces, i.e. they are **streamlined**.

- When two surfaces rub together, the force of **friction**:

  (i) Opposes the motion. For example, after they have opened their parachutes, parachutists slow down as they fall, until the upward force of air resistance is balanced by their weight and they then fall at a constant speed.

  (ii) Releases energy in the form of heat.

  For example:

  – Brake pads on cars and bicycles become hot as the force of friction between them and the moving wheel releases heat.

  – Boy scouts will rub two sticks together to generate enough heat to light a fire.

Changing shape – elastic bodies

ⓘ Bodies which are able to change shape when a force is exerted on them **and return** to their original shape when the force is removed, are said to be **elastic**.

Changing shapes of springs

This is usually done by measuring the **extension** of the spring when increasing force is applied.

extension = new length – original length

- The extension is **in proportion** to the loads applied **and** the spring returns to its original length when the force is removed – it is **elastic**.

- This feature of springs is why they are used in the construction of **newton meters**.

- The spring is elastic **until** a load is added which causes the spring not to return to its original length. The extension is now **not** in direct proportion to the load applied and the **elastic limit** of the spring has been exceeded.

Extensions of combinations of similar springs

ⓘ Springs in series:

total extension = extension of one spring x number of springs

Springs in parallel ('sharing the load – side by side'):

total extension = extension of one spring ÷ number of springs

13+

P

Turning forces – levers

- A lever is any **rigid** body which is able to turn about a **pivot**.

- Forces which cause levers to turn are called **turning moments**.

  turning moment (Nm) = size of force (N) x distance from pivot (m)

Balancing levers

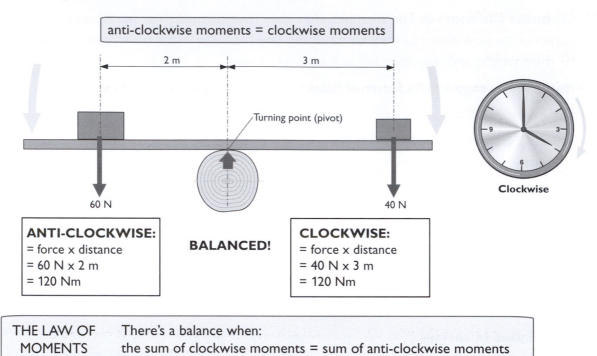

anti-clockwise moments = clockwise moments

2 m   3 m

Turning point (pivot)

60 N   40 N

Clockwise

ANTI-CLOCKWISE:
= force x distance
= 60 N x 2 m
= 120 Nm

BALANCED!

CLOCKWISE:
= force x distance
= 40 N x 3 m
= 120 Nm

THE LAW OF MOMENTS	There's a balance when: the sum of clockwise moments = sum of anti-clockwise moments

- A smaller force is able to balance a larger force.
- The smaller force is **further away** from the pivot than the larger force.

This is why:

- It is easier to dig soil with a long-handled spade rather than a short-handled trowel.
- Door handles are placed as far away from the hinges (pivot) as possible.
- Long door handles are easier to turn than door knobs.

Combining levers

- Scissors, pliers and wire cutters are all two levers which turn about the same pivot.

- The force you exert is called the **effort** and the force exerted, i.e. does the cutting, is called the **load**.

- Cutting tools **always** have **longer handles** than blades. For example:
  – Garden shears for cutting hedges have longer handles than scissors used for cutting paper.
  – Tin snips used to cut metal sheets have longer handles than electrical wire cutters.

Pressure

- The force acting on **each** m² is known as **pressure**.

- To calculate the pressure exerted by one surface on another, we use the relationship:

  pressure = force applied/area (P = F/A)

- The unit of pressure is N/m².

- 1 N/m² is also called 1 pascal (Pa).

Pressure in action

Decreasing the area over which a force acts, **increases** the pressure. For example:

– Sports shoes – studs/spikes.

– Any sharp point or blade.

Increasing the area over which a force acts, **decreases** the pressure. For example:

– Tank/Caterpillar tracks.

– Skis, snow-shoes.

Sample questions

Try these sample questions for yourself. The answers are given at the back of the book.

6.12   On Earth, gravity exerts a force of 10 N/kg. Calculate the weight of the following masses:

   (a) 3 kg   (2)

   (b) 30 kg   (2)

   (c) 180 kg   (2)

   (d) 500 g   (2)

   (e) 320 g   (2)

6.13   On Earth, gravity exerts a force of 10 N/kg and the Moon exerts a force of 1.6 N/kg. An astronaut has a mass of 40 kg on Earth.

   (a) What is his mass on the Moon?   (2)

   (b) What is his weight on Earth?   (2)

   (c) What is his weight on the Moon?   (2)

6.14   Write down the word or words which best complete each of the following sentences.

   (a) If a force acts on a moving body in the same direction as the movement, then the body will . . . . in speed (i.e. . . . .).   (2)

13+

P

(b) If a force acts on a moving body in the opposite direction to the movement, then the body will .... in speed (i.e. slow down). (1)

(c) When the two opposing forces are equal (i.e. are balanced), the body will move at a .... (1)

6.15 You have seven springs that are all similar. You test one of them and find that it extends 8 cm when a load of 100 g is applied.

(a) What would be the total extension if you connect three of them together in series and put on a load of 200 g? (2)

(b) What would be the total extension if you connect four of them together in parallel and put on a load of 200 g? (2)

6.16 A man turns a nut by exerting a force of 300 N at the end of a spanner which is 15 cm long. What is the turning moment applied to the nut? (2)

6.17 If a turning moment of 8 Nm were produced at a point 0.8 m from the hinge of a door, what force was used to achieve this? (2)

6.18 A boy of mass 40 kg sits 270 cm from the centre of a see-saw. A girl of mass 30 kg sits on the other side. Where must she sit to enable the see-saw to balance? (2)

6.19 A box has a weight of 60 N. Write down what pressure it will exert on the ground if the area of the base is:

(a) 10 cm² (2)

(b) 12 cm² (2)

(c) 0.06 cm² (2)

6.20 A block weighs 100 N and exerts a pressure of 25 N/cm² when placed on a table. What is the area of the box in contact with the table? (2)

6.4 Light and sound

Light

ⓘ Light rays are electromagnetic waves which have been emitted by a **luminous source**; for example the Sun, a lamp, a flame when substances burn.

Features of light rays

1. They are **very fast** – at present nothing is known to travel faster and their speed through a vacuum is 300 000 000 m/s (usually written as 3.0×10^8 m/s).

2. They **travel in straight lines** – you cannot see round corners.

3. They will not travel through **opaque** materials – **shadows** are formed.

4. They can be **absorbed** (important when looking at the colour of objects) and **emitted** (radiated out by luminous sources).

Reflection of light

● When light rays hit a surface, they may bounce off it – this is **reflection**.

● **Smooth surfaces** (e.g. mirrors) reflect **all** of the light in **one direction**.

● **Rough surfaces** (e.g. paper) reflect the light in **many directions** – the light has been **scattered**.

How plane mirrors reflect light

● A **plane** mirror is one which is **flat**.

● The **normal** is an **imaginary** line at 90° to the surface of the mirror which is used for measuring angles.

● Rays coming from a light source **to the mirror** are called **incident rays** and they hit the mirror at the **angle of incidence**.

● Rays bouncing **away from the mirror** are called **reflected rays** and they move away at the **angle of reflection**.

angle of incidence = angle of reflection

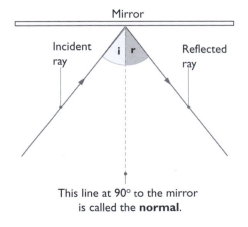

i = angle of incidence
r = angle of reflection

Note: When using a protractor to measure these angles, place the baseline of your protractor along the normal.

This line at 90° to the mirror is called the **normal**.

137

Using mirrors

The periscope

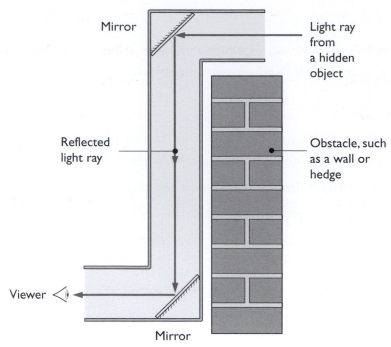

Refraction of light

Light will travel at different speeds, depending on what it is travelling through. For example:

Medium travelling through	Speed of light
Air	3.0×10^8 m/s
Water	2.25×10^8 m/s
Glass	2.0×10^8 m/s

- When light travels **from air into water**, **it slows down** and **bends towards** the normal.

- When light travels **from water into air**, **it speeds up** and **bends away from** the normal.

- The bending of light as it reaches the boundary between different materials is called **refraction**.

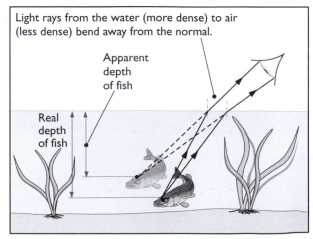

Colour

- Sir Isaac Newton shone a beam of white light through a prism and found that it split up into all the colours of the rainbow with the colours in the following order:

red – orange – yellow – green – blue – indigo – violet

✓ To help you remember the order of the colours, use the phrase:

Richard Of York Gave Battle In Vain.

- The display on a screen resulting from the splitting of white light into its colours is called a **spectrum**.

- In the case of white light, the colours run into each other, forming a **continuous spectrum** – such as you can see in a rainbow.

- The splitting of white light into its colours is called **dispersion**.

- Raindrops act as little prisms and disperse white sunlight into the colours that we see as a rainbow.

Refraction of red and blue light

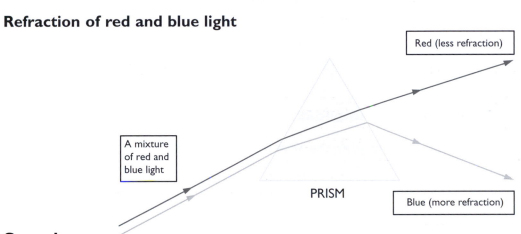

A mixture of red and blue light

Red (less refraction)

Blue (more refraction)

PRISM

Sound

Sound waves

- If you clamp a hacksaw blade at one end, pull up and release the other end it will move up and down in a series of **vibrations**.

- Vibrations are carried through the air as **longitudinal sound waves**.

- Sound waves are made up of sequences of:

compression – rarefaction – compression ... and so on

   – As the blade moves **down** it **squashes** the air below – **compression**.

   – As the blade moves **up** it **stretches** the air below – **rarefaction**.

- Sound waves **cannot** travel through a **vacuum**.

   – Sound waves need 'something' to squash and stretch, so can only travel through substances that contain atoms and/or molecules.

   – There are **no** atoms and/or molecules in a **vacuum**.

Speed of sound waves

The speed of sound waves depends upon the material (**medium**) through which they travel.

Medium	Speed (in m/s)
Gases (air)	330
Liquids (water)	1500
Solids (metal)	5000

Sound waves travel much slower than light waves

Medium (air)	Speed (in m/s)
Light waves	300 000 000
Sound waves	330

- Light waves are **a million times faster** than sound waves.
  - This is why we **see** lightning **before** we **hear** the thunder clap.

Loudness of sound

- The size of the vibration is called its **amplitude**.

- The **greater** the **amplitude**, the **louder** the sound.

Why sounds become softer the further you are away

- Vibrations send out sound waves in **all directions**.

- Sound waves spread the energy from the vibrations over a **wider area** as they travel further from the vibrating source.

- Energy of the vibrations that reach the ear become less.
  - This is why we **see** cars on a distant motorway, even though we cannot **hear** them.

Pitch of sound

- The **number** of complete vibrations in a specified time (cycles per second) is called the **frequency**.

- A faster vibration (i.e. **higher frequency**) produces a sound which has a **higher** note, or more correctly a note of a **higher pitch**.

ⓘ **A high frequency of vibration results in a note of high pitch.**

A low frequency of vibration results in a note of low pitch.

13+

P

- **Frequency** is measured in **Hertz (Hz)**.

- Frequencies audible to the human ear are in the range of 20–20 000Hz.

- Dogs and bats are able to hear sounds of frequency of over 100 000 Hz – these sounds are inaudible to the human ear.

How we hear

Vibrations caused by sound waves cause the **eardrum** to vibrate.

$\downarrow$

These vibrations are passed on to the inner ear.

$\downarrow$

The inner ear changes vibrations into electrical messages that are taken to and sorted out into sounds by the **brain**.

Problems caused by loud sounds

- **Temporary deafness** will occur if the **eardrum** is perforated by loud bangs. Deafness is temporary because the eardrum is able to repair itself.

- **Permanent deafness** might occur because of damage done to the inner ear by very loud sounds.

- Loud sounds speed up damage to the ear. This results in reducing the range of frequencies that can be heard.

Sample questions

Try these sample questions for yourself. The answers are given at the back of the book.

6.21 Light rays are emitted from a luminous source. List three other facts about light rays. (3)

6.22 (a) What is refraction? (1)

(b) When does this happen? (1)

(c) Why does this happen? (1)

6.23 (a) Using two mirrors, design an instrument for looking over a high garden fence. (4)

(b) What is the name of your instrument? (1)

6.24 The speed of sound in air is about 300 m/s. If thunder is heard 10 seconds after the lightning is seen, how far away is the storm? (2)

6.25 A man fires a gun and hears the echo from a building 550 m away. If the speed of sound in air is 330 m/s, how long after firing the gun will he hear the echo? (2)

6.26 (a) What feature of a sound wave determines the (i) pitch, (ii) loudness, of a note? (2)

(b) Use the features you have described in (a) to describe two differences between a high, loud note and a low, quiet one. (2)

6.5 The Earth and beyond

See Chapter 5, Section 5.4, pages 116–117 for the Earth's place in the solar system and how we experience day and night.

Reasons for the seasons

- The Earth's axis is not vertical, but is tilted by about 23°. This means that at any one time, part of the Earth's surface is closer to the Sun than others.

	Height of Sun	Temperature of Earth's surface	Length of shadow	Length of day
Summer	High	Warm	Short	Long
Winter	Low	Cold	Long	Short

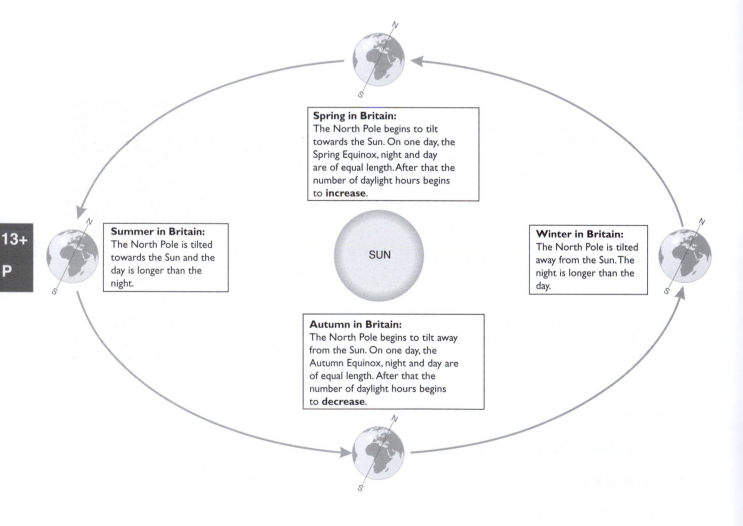

Spring in Britain:
The North Pole begins to tilt towards the Sun. On one day, the Spring Equinox, night and day are of equal length. After that the number of daylight hours begins to **increase**.

Summer in Britain:
The North Pole is tilted towards the Sun and the day is longer than the night.

SUN

Winter in Britain:
The North Pole is tilted away from the Sun. The night is longer than the day.

Autumn in Britain:
The North Pole begins to tilt away from the Sun. On one day, the Autumn Equinox, night and day are of equal length. After that the number of daylight hours begins to **decrease**.

Eclipse of the Moon (lunar eclipse)

● Happens when the **Earth** is between the **Moon** and the **Sun**.

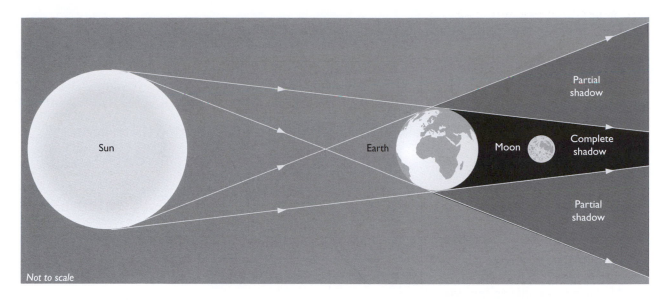

Not to scale

Eclipse of the Sun (solar eclipse)

● Happens when the **Moon** is between the **Earth** and the **Sun**.

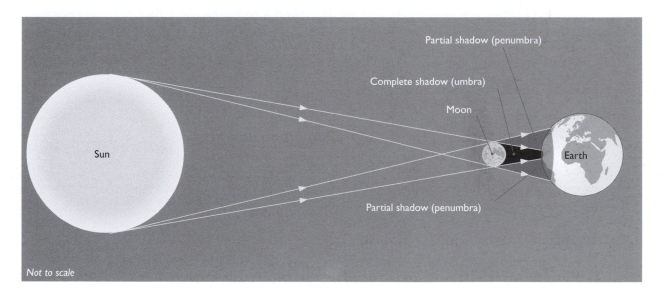

Not to scale

Our place in the Universe

● Within the **Universe** there are over 100 billion **galaxies**.

● A **galaxy** is the name given to a group of stars. A galaxy contains over 100 000 stars.

● We are located on the edge of a galaxy (called the **Milky Way**) which is so huge, it takes light 100 000 years to cross it.

● We say that the distance across the Milky Way is 100 000 light years.

- A **light year** is the **distance** that light (travelling at 3×10^5 km/s) travels in **one year**. (It comes to 9×10^{12} km or about **600 000** times greater than the distance from the Earth to the Sun.)

- Our nearest star (called Alpha Centauri) is about 4.2 light years away.

ⓘ We can see **stars** because they are **luminous sources and give out light**.

We see **planets** because they **reflect light from the Sun**.

The planets in our Solar System are held in their orbits by **gravitational attraction** between them and the **Sun**.

Satellites

- A satellite is something that orbits a larger body in the Solar System. Their **forward motion** and **gravitational force** keeps them in **orbit**.

- **Natural satellites** include:

  Planets orbiting the Sun.

  The Moon orbiting the Earth.

- **Artificial satellites** are man-made and are launched into space for a particular purpose. For example:

  – Observation of the Earth for weather forecasting; geological surveys.

  – Observation for military purposes.

  – Communications: satellite TV, radio, mobile phones.

  – Observing space: e.g. Hubble telescope.

Sample questions

Try these sample questions for yourself. The answers are given at the back of the book.

6.27 What causes us to have seasons on Earth? (2)

6.28 Write the words that complete the following sentences:

(a) An eclipse of the Moon (lunar eclipse) happens when the . . . . is between the Moon and the . . . . (2)

(b) An eclipse of the Sun (solar eclipse) happens when the . . . . is between the . . . . and the Sun. (2)

6.29 What does the term **light year** refer to? (1)

6.30 The Hubble telescope operates from a satellite. Why should this provide better pictures of space than land-based telescopes? (2)

6.6 Energy

Work and energy

> ⓘ If **anything** happens, then **energy has been supplied**.
>
> For **anything** to happen, a supply of **energy is needed**.

What is 'anything'?

Another description could be 'job'. Examples of jobs include:

– An animal moving, eating, living.

– A kettle heating water.

– A battery of cells making a radio produce sound.

The size of the job (called **work**) can be measured and the unit of work is called the **joule (J)**.

As we cannot measure energy as such, we measure the amount of **work** done.

Work is done when (i) a force produces motion; (ii) something is heated.

Clearly, more work will have been done if:

● You run 200 m instead of 50 m.

● You boil 2000 cm^3 of cold water rather than 250 cm^3.

amount of work done (J) = amount of energy supplied (J)

So the unit we use to measure **energy** is the **joule (1000 J = 1 kJ)**.

> ⓘ Energy is:
>   work that has been done OR work that is able to be done.

Forms of energy

Kinetic energy (KE)

● This is energy which a body has **because it is moving**.

● The amount of **kinetic energy** which a body has depends upon two factors:

  (i) The **mass (m)** of the moving object.

  (ii) The **speed (v)** of the moving body.

Potential energy (PE)

● This is energy which a body has because of its **position** or **condition**.

● PE is a measure of work which is **able to be** done.

Gravitational potential energy (GPE)

– A 'bomb' jump from a diving board will make a **bigger** splash if done from a **higher** board.

– A **large** adult will make a **bigger** splash when doing the same jump than a **smaller** youth.

– In **both** cases, the jumpers fall **because** gravity pulls their masses downwards towards the Earth's centre.

ⓘ The amount of **gravitational potential energy** that a body has depends upon three factors:

(i)   The **mass (m)** of the body.

(ii) The **vertical height (h)** which the body falls – or can fall.

(iii) The **force of gravity (g)** acting on the body.

Elastic potential energy (strain energy)

– Winding up a clockwork toy; the more turns you make, the further/faster the toy will move.

– The number of turns is a measure of the strain put on the spring and is the equivalent of the '**h**' as seen in GPE.

– Pulling back the string of a bow to shoot an arrow; the further you pull back, the more the bow is under strain and the further the arrow will fly as the bow returns to its original shape.

– The distance you pull the string (from its normal 'resting' position) is the equivalent of '**h**' as seen in GPE.

– More and more energy is stored in the bow as it bends and changes shape more and more.

Chemical energy

● When chemicals react, they change and form **new** substances.

● During chemical change, energy is released.

For example:

– Burning magnesium will change **chemical energy** into **radiation energy** (heat and light).

– The chemicals of an electric cell will, when a circuit is complete, change **chemical energy** into **electrical energy**.

Electrical energy

- Electric currents move energy from one place to another.

- **When things move, work is done** and so energy has been used.

- This energy is used to make other things happen.

  For example:

  – A lamp shining (called the **heating effect** of a current).

  – A motor turning (called the **magnetic effect** of a current).

  – A chemical compound decomposing (called the **chemical effect** of a current).

Thermal energy (heat)

- **All** matter consists of molecules which are constantly in motion (i.e. have KE).

- If you add together the KE of all the molecules, the **sum** is called the **internal energy** of the substance.

- Adding energy (heating) increases the KE of the molecules, so the **internal energy rises**.

- The rise in internal energy can be detected by a rise in **temperature**.

So, the form of energy which brings about a rise in internal energy and, hence, temperature of a substance, is known as **thermal energy** (sometimes this has also been known as heat energy).

ⓘ **Heating and cooling**

- Thermal energy **tends** to flow from a warm place to a colder one.

- Bodies which **absorb** energy, become **warmer**.

- Bodies which **emit (lose)** energy, become **cooler**.

13+

P

Sound energy

Vibrating bodies will give out energy in the form of sound waves that are able to travel through solids, liquids and gases, but not through a vacuum (see Section 6.4, page 139).

Light energy

Energy from the Sun is carried by **electromagnetic waves**. One of the many types of electromagnetic waves are **light waves**.

- Light waves enable us to see objects (see Section 6.4, page 137).

- Light waves are absorbed by plants and provide the energy for the chemical reactions which change water and carbon dioxide into sugar and oxygen (photosynthesis).

Changing energy from one form to another

- When we say that we are **using** energy, we are really **changing** energy from one form to another.

- Energy is **never used up**, it changes from **one form to another**.

- The process of changing energy from one form to another is called **transferring** energy.

- A **transducer** is anything that will change energy from one form to another.

- We can list the transferring of energy from one form to another in an **energy chain**.

- In an energy chain listing energy transfers, **heat is always** at the end of the list.

Form of energy at start	Transducer	Form/s of energy at end
Electrical	Lamp	Heat, light
Chemical	Cell	Electrical, heat
Chemical	Bunsen burner	Heat, light, sound
Sound	Microphone	Electrical, heat
Electrical	Loudspeaker	Sound, heat
Electrical	Motor	Kinetic, sound, heat
Kinetic	Dynamo/generator	Electrical, sound, heat
Light	Solar cell	Electrical, heat

ⓘ **Law of Conservation of Energy**

When energy changes form:

total amount of energy at the start = total amount of energy at the end

There are **no exceptions** to this law.

Energy cannot be used twice

- A lamp changes **electrical energy** into **heat** and **light**.

- Light is 'useful'; heat is 'wasted' – **both** are radiated out into space and cannot be used again.

- If 10 J of energy are used to light a lamp, we will not obtain 10 J's worth of light, as much of the energy will be 'wasted' in the form of heat as the lamp warms.

Where does energy come from?

ⓘ The Sun is our main supply of energy.

The Sun is a **renewable source of energy**, as energy from the Sun will be radiated for the foreseeable future. A renewable source is one that can be replenished within a lifetime.

Most of the Earth's energy comes from the Sun.

For example:

— Direct heat rays from the Sun can be collected and focused in one place, as in a **solar furnace**.

— Radiation from the Sun can be changed into electrical energy by a **solar cell**.

— Plants use radiation from the Sun as the supply of energy for photosynthesis which changes carbon dioxide and water into oxygen and sugars and starch which **increases biomass** and is a supply of **chemical energy**. This supply of chemical energy can be used:

(i) As a source of food: changed into thermal energy as animals respire and do work.

(ii) In the production of fuel. For example:

— Wood: an important fuel.

— Production of methane: from rotting vegetation.

— Production of alcohol: from sugar plants which are allowed to ferment.

Radiation from the Sun causes some parts of the Earth to become hotter than others.

This results in **convection currents** being set up in oceans and the atmosphere.

These currents drive the winds and waves, changing the Sun's radiated energy into **kinetic energy**. **This is also called wind/wave energy**.

Radiation from the Sun causes water to evaporate from oceans and lakes.

The evaporated water rises, is carried by winds and may fall as rain on high ground. Now the water has **gravitational potential energy**.

As the water falls back to the sea, its gravitational potential energy is changed to **kinetic energy** which enables the water to:

— Wear away the mountainside: erosion.

— Turn a water wheel: e.g. a flour mill.

— Turn a turbine: hydroelectricity. This is also called **falling water energy**.

The Sun is also the initial supply of energy for the **fossil fuels**, which are **non-renewable** sources of energy.

Electricity may be generated using renewable or non-renewable resources.

Renewable resources

- Are either constantly available or can be replaced rapidly.

- Cause little or no atmospheric pressure.

- Are often expensive to exploit.

- May not be reliable, e.g. wind energy, wave energy, solar energy.

Hydroelectric power station

– **Water** rushes at **great speed** past turbine blades which turn, causing the rotor to turn.

Wind power

– The blades of a wind turbine are giant propellers that are located high in the air to catch as much wind as possible.

– Many wind turbines are located together in what are called 'wind farms'.

Geothermal power

– The temperature of the Earth's centre is about 4000 °C.

– Electricity can be generated from the hot water or steam from the hot interior of the Earth.

Solar power

– Light energy from the Sun can be changed into electricity by **solar cells**.

– Each cell produces a small amount of electricity, so a large number of these are required to make a useful amount.

– The effectiveness of these relies on a plentiful supply of sunlight.

Tidal power

– Rotation of the Earth, together with gravitational forces between the Earth and Moon, cause the water of the oceans to be pulled into 'heaps' resulting in high tides about twice a day.

– Water which is trapped at high tide has gravitational potential energy and this can be changed to kinetic energy and used to drive turbines.

Wave power

– The constant up and down movement of a sea wave can be changed into rotary motion which is used to turn a rotor to generate electricity.

Nuclear power

– Energy is produced when the nuclei of atoms are changed, for example when atoms are split.

Biomass

– Heat is created by burning wood or other plant material.

Non-renewable resources (fossil fuels)

- Fossil fuels do not become useful until the stored energy within them is released by combining them with oxygen when they burn.

- Once fossil fuels have burned, they **cannot be used again**.

- Fossil fuels are also used as raw materials in the manufacture of many substances (plastics, medicines, cosmetics). A world without oil does not merely affect the motor car!

- It has taken over 100 million years to form coal, gas and oil and it is likely that we will have taken a few hundred years to use up supplies of these.

- Burning fossil fuels releases polluting gases such as carbon dioxide and sulphur dioxide into the atmosphere.

- Electricity can be produced more reliably and cheaply in fossil fuel-burning power stations than by using renewable resources.

Thermal power station

- When a coil (**rotor**) turns inside a magnet (**stator**), a current of electricity is produced.

- The coil (**rotor**) is located on the **same revolving axle** as a set of turbines.
  – Steam at high pressure turns the turbine and rotor.
  – In order to change water into steam, water can be **heated** using **coal**, **oil**, **gas** or **uranium** (in a nuclear reactor).

Coal

- Between 100 and 600 million years ago **plants** absorbed energy from the Sun and, through photosynthesis, 'stored' this energy in the form of sugars and starch.

- As plants died and fell into the swamps, the chemical energy stayed 'locked' within them.

- Over a period of at least 100 million years, sediments were laid on top of the plant remains. Pressure increased as more layers were laid on top and the plants hardened and became rock-like (**fossils**), changing into **coal**.

Oil and gas

- Formed between 100 and 500 million years ago from small plants and **animals** living in the **oceans**.

- When they died, they sank to the ocean bed and were covered with layers of mud and sediments.

- Over the following millions of years, the decomposed plants and animals changed into **oil** and **gas**.

13+

P

Sample questions

Try these sample questions for yourself. The answers are given at the back of the book.

6.31 (a) What does the word 'work' mean? (1)

(b) What is the unit used to measure work? (1)

(c) What is the relationship between work and energy? (2)

6.32 What does the Law of Conservation of Energy state? (2)

6.33 Complete the table below. (11)

Form of energy at start	Transducer	Form/s of energy at end
Electrical	. . . .	. . . . , light
. . . .	Cell	Electrical, heat
Chemical	Bunsen burner	. . . . , ... , ...
Sound	Microphone	. . . . , heat
. . . .	Loudspeaker	Sound, heat
Electrical	Motor	. . . . , sound, heat
. . . .	Dynamo/generator	Electrical, sound, heat
Light	. . . .	Electrical, heat

6.34 (a) What does the term 'fossil fuel' mean? (2)

(b) Name two fossil fuels. (2)

(c) Why are fossil fuels called non-renewable? (2)

(d) Is burning the only use of fossil fuels? (2)

6.35 It is possible to buy household electric lamps which are said to be more efficient than 'normal' ones.

(a) Into which two forms of energy is electrical energy changed by a normal lamp? (2)

(b) If a lamp is more efficient, which of the energy forms is likely to be reduced? (1)

6.36 A cord is wrapped round the axle of a dynamo/generator on a bench. A mass is tied to the cord and allowed to fall. The dynamo is connected to a lamp which lights as the mass is falling. List the energy changes taking place as the mass falls. (6)

6.37 Body temperature is 37°C and room temperature is 20°C. A cup of tea is 60°C. Why does a warm cup of tea feel cold to drink when it has been standing for about 15 minutes? (3)

Summary

You should now know the following:

1. The difference between mass and weight.

2. How to measure the volume of different objects and substances.

3. How to calculate the density of different substances.

4. The main features of electric circuits and their different components.

5. The effects of forces and motion.

6. The main features of light rays, including what happens to light during reflection and refraction.

7. The main features of sound waves, including loudness and pitch.

8. The effects of the Moon and the Sun on the Earth.

9. The main features of the different forms of energy.

10. How electricity is generated.

Use the glossary at the back of the book for definitions of key words.

Test yourself

Make sure you can answer the following questions. The answers are at the back of the book.

1. Suggest what apparatus and units you would use to measure the following:

   (a) The height of a Bunsen burner.

   (b) The mass of an apple.

   (c) The volume of a wooden pencil box.

   (d) The volume of water left in your water bottle.

   (e) The volume of a small bunch of keys.

2. How many boxes of drawing pins, each measuring 2 cm x 3 cm x 0.5 cm, can you fit into a box measuring 60 cm x 30 cm x 15 cm?

3. The density of water is 1 g/cm³. What is the mass of water in a box which measures 30 cm x 50 cm x 20 cm?

4. Draw a circuit which has one cell and one switch, which will light two lamps to 'normal' brightness.

5. Write down the equation used to calculate the weight of a body. Include all units.

6. A spring is 6 cm long. When a load of 100 g is attached to it, the new length is 8 cm. It returns to 6 cm when the load is removed.

What will be the length when:

(a) A load of 50 g is attached?

(b) A load of 75 g is attached?

7. Write down **two** features of a lever.

8. A ray of light hits a mirror at an angle.

(a) What is the name of this ray?

(b) What happens to it after it has hit the mirror?

(c) What is this process called?

9. Draw a diagram to show how you would split a ray of light that was a mixture of red and blue light, into its separate colours.

10. Complete the following table:

	Height of Sun	Temperature of Earth's surface	Length of shadow	Length of day
Summer				
Winter				

11. Put in ascending order:

| star   universe   planet   solar system   galaxy |

12. What is energy?

13. List five different forms of energy.

Glossary

Anther	Part of the stamen, the male part of a flower.
Arteries	Blood vessels which carry blood away from the heart.
Brain	An organ found in the head which controls many of the life processes in animals.
Canines	Killing teeth which are well developed in carnivores.
Carbohydrates	A food substance, including starches and sugars, which supplies most of the energy we need.
Carnivore	An animal that eats other animals.
Carpel	The female part of a flower – made up of stigma, style and ovary.
Chlorophyll	A green pigment (colour) in plant cells that can absorb light energy in photosynthesis.
Consumer	An organism in a food chain that eats other organisms.
Embryo root	Part of the plant seed which grows out of the seed during germination to anchor the young plant in the soil and absorb water.
Embryo shoot	Part of the plant seed which grows out of the seed during germination to form the stem and leaves.
Fats	A food substance providing a supply of energy.
Fertilisation	The joining together of male and female sex cells.
Fibre	A substance that comes from plants which provides bulk to our food to enable it to travel through the digestive system more efficiently.
Filament	Part of the stamen, the male part of a flower.
Flower	Part of the plant containing the reproductive organs.
Food store	Part of the plant seed which provides the first raw materials for the growth of the young plant.
Germination	The change from a seed to a young plant.
Growth	A life process where an organism increases in size.
Heart	An organ that pumps blood through all parts of an animal's body.
Herbivore	An animal that eats plants.
Hibernation	A way of avoiding harsh conditions by sleeping for a long period.

Incisors	Cutting teeth in the front of the jaw.
Intestines	A long tube that runs from the stomach to the anus and breaks the food down, so that useful substances can be taken into the blood.
Invertebrate	An animal without a backbone.
Kidneys	Organs which keep the body free of impurities, removing excess water from the blood, filtering out impurities made by the body and creating waste liquid called urine.
Leaf	Part of the plant which traps sunlight.
Liver	An organ in the body which deals with food taken in by the intestines; it stores some useful parts of food and makes a lot of heat which helps keep the body warm.
Lungs	Organs that allow oxygen to enter the body.
Migration	A way of avoiding harsh conditions by moving to a new habitat.
Mineral salts	Substances that usually combine with another food to form different parts of the body, such as teeth, bones (from calcium) and red blood cells (from iron).
Molars	Grinding teeth at the side of the jaw.
Nocturnal	Being active at night, like an owl.
Nutrients	The food substances required to carry out the processes which are essential for life.
Nutrition	The life process that provides a living organism with its food.
Obesity	An extremely heavy body weight that might cause illness.
Omnivore	An animal that eats plants and animals.
Ovary	Part of the carpel, the female part of a flower.
Ovule	The part of the plant's ovary that contains the egg cell.
Oxygen	The gas required by all living organisms in order to burn up food for energy.
Photosynthesis	A plant nutrition process that uses light energy to change carbon dioxide gas and water into food and oxygen.
Plaque	A sticky mixture of bacteria and sugar that can lead to tooth decay.
Pollination	The transfer of the male sex cell, or pollen grain, from the anther to the stigma of a flower.
Predator	An animal that hunts and captures other animals.
Pre-molars	Scissor-like teeth in carnivores, to tear and grind food.

Prey	An animal hunted and captured by other animals.
Protein	A food substance used in the growth and repair of cells.
Pulse	The stretching of artery walls caused by the beating of the heart.
Reproduction	The life process that produces new individual organisms.
Roots	The part of a plant which absorbs water and minerals from the soil; they also anchor the plant firmly in the soil.
Seed	What develops if an ovule is fertilised.
Skeleton	The bony structure of the body (including the skull, collarbone, shoulder blade, ribcage and pelvis) which supports the tissues and organs and enables movement to take place.
Stamen	The male part of a flower.
Stamina	The ability to keep working or exercising for a long time.
Stem	The part of the plant which supports the leaves, holding them up towards the light.
Stigma	A part of the carpel, the female part of a flower.
Stomach	A part of the body which stores food, and churns and mixes it up with chemicals helping to break it down.
Style	A part of the carpel, the female part of a flower.
Veins	Blood vessels that carry blood back to the heart.
Vertebrate	An animal with a backbone (as part of a bony skeleton).
Vitamins	Substances needed in very small amounts to enable the body to use other nutrients more efficiently: for example vitamin C, which is crucial in avoiding bleeding gums and loose teeth.
Water	The liquid formed from a combination of hydrogen and oxygen and required by all living organisms in order to survive.

13+ Biology

Aerobic respiration	The form of respiration involving air.
Antagonistic muscles	A pair of muscles which have opposite actions enabling movement to take place.
Arthropods	The class of animal which has jointed limbs, a hard outer body covering and segmented body.
Bacteria	Cells that live and grow outside living cells.

Carbon cycle	A series of chemical reactions that follow what happens to carbon dioxide, oxygen, water and sugars in the environment – it links photosynthesis and respiration.
Cell surface membrane	The part of a cell surrounding the cytoplasm.
Competition	Two or more organisms trying to obtain the same thing from their environment.
Cytoplasm	The living material of a cell, other than the nucleus.
DNA	Genetic material contained within the nucleus of a cell.
Egestion	The process of removing waste material from the body.
Enzymes	Chemicals that enable other chemical reactions to happen.
Fetus	A developing baby in the womb.
Food chain/web	The passage of food energy between different living organisms – made up of producers and consumers.
Fungi	One of the five kingdoms of living organisms which has similar cells to plants but is unable to carry out photosynthesis.
Gamete	The male and female sex cells.
Genes	Coded information contained within the nucleus of a cell which determines how a cell replicates itself.
Glucose	The sugar obtained from digested food which reacts with oxygen in respiration.
Nucleus	The control centre of a cell, containing the genetic material.
Ovum	A cell containing the female genes.
Predation	When animals hunt and capture other animals. This will affect the size of the population.
Respiration	The release of energy for life processes.
Single-celled organism	One of the five kingdoms of living organisms where the organism has a single cell with a nucleus.
Sperm	A cell containing the male genes.
Starch	A type of carbohydrate which is stored in the muscles and liver in humans and is the food store in many plant tissues.
Viruses	Microbes that invade living cells in order to reproduce.
Zygote	The fertilised egg produced when gametes are joined together during fertilisation.

11+ Chemistry

Boiling	A physical change in which heat changes a liquid into a gas, e.g. liquid water into water vapour.
Condensing	A physical change in which cooling a gas changes it into a liquid.
Conductor	A material that allows something to pass through it, e.g. a metal wire is a conductor because it allows electricity to pass through it.
Decanting	A way of separating a solid from a liquid by letting the solid settle and then pouring the liquid into another container.
Evaporating	A physical process in which a liquid changes into a gas.
Filtrate	The liquid that passes through a filter.
Filtration	A process that uses a filter (like a sieve) to separate a solid from a liquid.
Fossil fuel	A fuel that was made millions of years ago from the bodies of dead animals and plants.
Freezing	The change of a liquid into a solid as the temperature falls, e.g. liquid water changing to ice. This is also known as solidifying.
Humus	A sticky material in soil made by the decay of dead animals and plants.
Insoluble	Something which will not dissolve in a liquid, e.g. sand is insoluble in water.
Insulator	A material that does not allow heat/electricity to pass through it, e.g. polystyrene, because it does not let heat pass through it.
Loam	A soil for growing plants, with an ideal mixture of rock particles, air, water, minerals and humus.
Magnet	A substance that can attract a metal such as iron.
Melting	A physical process in which heat changes a solid to a liquid, e.g. ice can melt into liquid water.
Metal	A material that may be hard, can be bent, polished and conducts heat and electricity. (A material that does not have these characteristics is called a non-metal.)
Residue	The material left on a filter when a mixture is poured through it.
Rusting	A process in which air and water cause a chemical change to iron.
Sieving	The process of using a mesh to separate a mixture of solid particles of different sizes.
Soluble	Able to dissolve in a liquid, e.g. salt is soluble in water.

Solute	A substance that can dissolve in a liquid (the solvent) to form a solution.
Solution	The mixture formed when a solute dissolves in a solvent.
Solvent	The liquid that can dissolve a solute to form a solution.
Water cycle	The change of water between solid, liquid and gas that circulates water around the planet Earth.

13+ Chemistry

Atom	The smallest particle of an element.
Boiling point	The temperature at which a liquid changes to a gas or a gas changes to a liquid.
Compound	A material formed from the chemical reaction of two or more elements.
Condensation	A physical change in which cooling a gas changes it into a liquid.
Decomposition	A chemical reaction in which one substance is broken down into several products.
Density	The amount of mass in a specified volume.
Dissolving	A process that spreads out particles of a solid through a liquid to produce a solution.
Distillation	The separation and recovery of a solvent from a solution.
Element	A material that is made up of one type of atom.
Litmus paper	Test papers used to detect the presence of acids or alkalis.
Melting point	The temperature at which a solid changes to a liquid or a liquid changes to a solid.
Molecule	A particle made from two or more atoms joined together.
Neutralisation	A chemical reaction between acids and alkalis, producing a neutral solution.
Oxidation	A chemical reaction where elements combine with oxygen to form compounds called oxides.
Periodic Table	A table of all the elements listed in order of their atomic number.
pH scale	A numbering system used to show the strengths of acids and alkalis.
Reactivity series	A list of metals showing how well they react with oxygen, water, steam and acids.

Reduction	A chemical reaction in which substances lose oxygen or gain hydrogen.
Sublimation	The change of state from solid to gas or gas to solid, missing out the liquid state.
Universal indicator	A liquid or test paper used to find the pH value of a solution, depending on the colour.

11+ Physics

Air resistance	The friction between an object and the air.
Attract	To pull together, e.g. opposite poles of a magnet attract each other.
Cell	A source of electricity in which chemical reactions produce electrical charge.
Circuit	Some electrical components arranged together, so that electric current can flow.
Force	Something causing (i) a stationary body to move and/or change shape; (ii) change in the speed or the direction of movement of a moving body. This can be a push, pull, support (reaction) or upthrust.
Friction	A force between two objects when they rub together.
Gravity	The force that pulls objects together (for example, gravity is the force that pulls us towards the centre of the Earth).
Loudness	A measure of the intensity of a sound – in other words, how much energy the sound has.
Luminous	Giving out light, e.g. the Sun is a luminous object.
Newton	A unit of force.
Opaque	Not allowing light to pass through.
Pitch	How high or low a sound is.
Poles	The two ends of a magnet; one end will be north-seeking and the other end south-seeking.
Repulsion	Pushing apart, e.g. like poles of a magnet repel each other.
Series circuit	A circuit with all the components connected one after another; there is no choice for the pathway of the current.
Shadow	An area behind an opaque object opposite a light source.
Translucent	Allowing light to pass through but creating a change in the light rays so that the image is unclear.

Transparent	Allowing light to pass through without changing the light rays, so that the image is clear.
Vacuum	A space with no particles in it.
Vibration	The movement of an object backward and forward, usually at high speed – there is no sound without vibration.

13+ Physics

AND circuit	A circuit with two switches connected in series so that the circuit will only work when both switches are on.
Chemical energy	The energy released when a chemical reaction takes place.
Electrical energy	The energy due to an electric current moving energy from one place to another.
Gravitational potential energy	The energy which a body has because of its position and its mass; the vertical height from which the body falls and the force of gravity.
Joule	The unit of energy.
Kinetic energy	The energy which a body has when it is moving.
Light energy	Energy carried by electromagnetic waves from luminous sources, e.g. from the Sun.
Light-dependent resistor	A component whose resistance will change depending on the intensity of light.
Light-emitting diode	A component that emits light when a small current flows through it.
OR circuits	A circuit with two switches connected in parallel so that the circuit will work when either switch is on.
Parallel circuits	Two or more individual circuits connected to the same electrical supply.
Pivot	The point around which something turns.
Refraction	The bending of light as it moves from one material to another one of different density.
Resistor	A component that is designed to reduce the current in a circuit.
Sound energy	Energy carried by sound waves.
Strain (elastic potential) energy	The energy which a body has, due to how much it has been bent or stretched.
Thermal energy	The energy due to the movement of the molecules inside a substance.
Weight	The force of gravity pulling an object downwards towards the Earth's centre.

Sample question answers

Chapter 1 (11+ Biology)

1.1   Cannot (i) reproduce, or (ii) grow.   (2)

1.2   Opening and closing of petals, flower heads following the path of the Sun.   (1)

1.3   To make sure that when an organism dies, there is another similar one to replace it.   (1)

1.4   An increase in the size and/or number of cells and is achieved by using the raw materials obtained through nutrition.   (2)

1.5   (4)

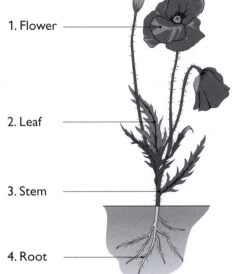

1. Flower

2. Leaf

3. Stem

4. Root

1.6   (7)

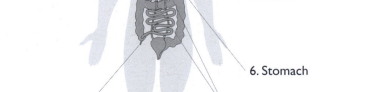

1. Lungs

4. Brain

2. Liver

5. Heart

6. Stomach

3. Intestines

7. Kidneys

1.7 The development of special features which enable an organism to survive in a particular environment. Example: a polar bear will have a very thick coat to help it withstand the low arctic temperatures. Pine needles on trees help reduce loss of water through evaporation. (2)

1.8

Type of tooth		Function	
Canine	(1)	Tearing of food and/or killing	(1)
Incisor	(1)	Cutting and biting of food	(1)
Pre-molar	(1)	Tearing and grinding of food	(1)
Molar	(1)	Crushing and grinding of food	(1)

1.9 (a) Bacteria in plaque change sugar in food into acid. The acid eats through the enamel causing decay. (1)

(b) Any three from: regular brushing; less sugar in diet; fluoride in toothpaste or water; regular dental visits. (3)

1.10 (a) Any two from: bread, bacon, orange juice. (2)

(b) Bacon, egg. (2)

(c) Any two from: vitamins, minerals, water, fibre. (2)

1.11 More energy is required so more food and oxygen is needed by the cells.
Lungs breathe faster so more oxygen can pass into the blood and the heart beats faster to take this extra oxygen and food to the cells. (2)

1.12 (a) The pulse rate would rise from normal at (i) to possibly much higher at (ii). (1)

(b) The pulse rate at (iii) will be lower that that at (ii), but not yet down to the normal level at (i). (2)

1.13 Support, protection, movement. (3)

1.14 (a) Needed to combine with food to release energy for life processes. (1)

(b) Needed to combine with water to make food during photosynthesis. (1)

1.15

Factor	Why the factor is important to healthy plant growth	
Air	Supply of oxygen and carbon dioxide	(1)
Light	Energy supply to make photosynthesis happen	(1)
Warmth	Right temperature to make all the chemical reactions in the plant happen at a satisfactory rate	(1)
Water	Raw material for photosynthesis; essential to maintain healthy firm cells	(1)
Minerals	Needed to combine with food, to make plant structures	(1)

1.16 (a) anthers; (b) ovules; (c) pollination; (d) fertilisation; (e) fruits; (f) germinate; (g) grow. (7)

1.17 (a) Any one from: attractive smell; display of bright/large petals. (1)

(b)

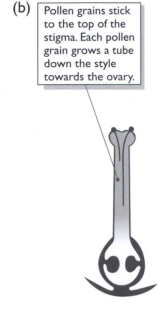

Pollen grains stick to the top of the stigma. Each pollen grain grows a tube down the style towards the ovary.

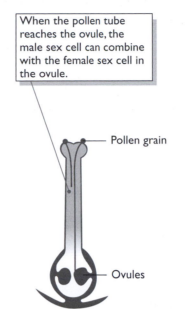

When the pollen tube reaches the ovule, the male sex cell can combine with the female sex cell in the ovule.

Pollen grain

Ovules (3)

1.18 (a) 2 and 3. (2)

(b) No; there is germination in 2 which is in the dark. (2)

(c) That oxygen is needed for germination to take place. (1)

1.19 See diagram on page 15. (5)

1.20 (a) Both are arthropods. (b) Spider has 8 legs, but fly has 6; spider has 2 body parts, but fly has 3; spider has no antennae, but a fly does. (2)

1.21

Invertebrate (no backbone)		Vertebrate (backbone)	
Octopus	(1)	Cat	(1)
Spider	(1)	Shark	(1)
Crab	(1)	Frog	(1)
Beetle	(1)	Fox	(1)

1.22 Lizard has a dry skin with scales; newt has a moist smooth skin. (2)

1.23 Any three from:

● Loss of agricultural land.

● Large-scale reduction of tropical rainforests.

● Reduction of fish stocks.

● Pollution of the air. (3)

1.24 Any three from:

- National parks, wild-life centres, zoos.

- Protection of 'endangered species'.

- More efficient engines to reduce harmful emissions when burning fossil fuels.

- Greater awareness of using 'alternative' forms of energy (wind, geothermal) to reduce pollution from burning of fossil fuels.

- Recycling of household waste to reduce landfill. (3)

1.25 (a) Any two from: coal, oil, gas. (2)

(b) They pollute the air causing acid rain. (2)

1.26 (a) (iv); (b) (iv); (c) (i); (d) (iii); (e) (ii). (5)

Chapter 2 (13+ Biology)

2.1   No. Root cells underground receive no light and do not carry out photosynthesis.   (2)

2.2   (a)   (2)

Ovum ●   ⚬ ⚬   Sperm

(b) The sperm has a tail for swimming. The egg cell is larger as it contains food for
the developing embryo after fertilisation. It is also not mobile.   (2)

(c) The sperm cell swims to the egg, and fertilisation takes place when the male
nucleus of the sperm fuses with the nucleus of the female egg to form a zygote.   (2)

2.3

Name of system	What it does	Main organs in the system
Locomotion	Supports the body and allows movement (1)	Muscles and skeleton of bones (1)
Transport	Takes food to all parts of body and removes waste from them (1)	Heart and blood vessels (1)
Respiratory	Provides oxygen and removes carbon dioxide from body (1)	Windpipe and lungs (1)
Nervous	Takes messages to/from all parts of the body via the brain (1)	Brain, spinal cord, nerves, eyes, ears, nose, tongue (1)
Digestive	Breaks down food and absorbs useful chemicals into the blood (1)	Gut, stomach, intestine, liver (1)
Reproductive	Produces/receives gametes for next generation (1)	Testes, ovaries, uterus (1)
Excretory	Removal of waste products (1)	Kidneys, bladder, liver (1)

2.4   (a) Either bread, bacon or orange juice.   (1)

(b) Bacon and egg.   (2)

(c) (i) Sugar; (ii) starch.   (2)

(d) Any two from: water, vitamins, minerals, fibre.   (2)

2.5   At 18, protein will be required mainly for growth. At 45, growth is completed, so
protein is required for repair and replacement of worn out cells.   (4)

2.6   (a) (i) Y. (ii) Although it is mainly indigestible, it provides bulk to enable food to pass
through the digestive system more efficiently.   (2)

(b) (i) X. (ii) Contains more carbohydrate for quick energy release and therefore a
greater supply of energy for the activity to come.   (2)

2.7   Vitamins:

- Vitamin C: tissue repair, resistance to disease, e.g. scurvy (bleeding gums).

- Vitamin A: growth, eyesight.   (2)

Minerals:

- Calcium: making of bones and teeth.

- Iron: making of red blood cells.   (2)

2.8   Support of tissues and organs; protection of delicate organs; enable movement.   (3)

2.9   (a) Because muscles never push. One muscle from the pair contracts, pulling the
          bone in a certain direction, whilst the opposite muscle relaxes. The reverse
          happens to move the bone back to where it was.   (2)

      (b) Biceps and triceps (move the lower arm).   (1)

      (c) Antagonistic muscles.   (1)

2.10 (a) To protect the brain from physical knocks.   (1)

      (b) To protect the spinal cord.   (1)

      (c) To protect the heart and lungs; to make the lungs bigger and smaller during breathing.   (1)

2.11 (a) Calcium phosphate.   (1)

      (b) A spongy material located in the centre of the bone where new bone cells
          (and red blood cells) are formed.   (2)

2.12 (a) In the oviduct (fallopian tube).   (1)

      (b) (i) The wall breaks down and passes out of the vagina.   (1)

          (ii) Menstruation or 'having a period'.   (1)

          (iii) Menstrual cycle.   (1)

          (iv) 28 days.   (1)

2.13 (a) Either carbon dioxide or (nitrogenous) waste, e.g. urea.   (1)

      (b) Oxygen and food.   (2)

2.14 The mother may have an entirely different blood group from the fetus – these must
      never mix. The mother's blood pressure will be much higher than that of the fetus.   (2)

2.15 Any two from:

- Carried inside the body.

- Protected by the thick walls of the uterus.

- Surrounded by protective fluid contained within the amniotic sac.   (2)

2.16 (a) The chemical reactions that release energy from foods.   (2)

      (b) In every living cell.   (1)

2.17 (a) $\boxed{\text{Glucose + oxygen}} \rightarrow \boxed{\text{carbon dioxide + water + energy}}$ (6)

(b) That air (oxygen) is required for the reaction to take place. (1)

2.18 (a) In the air sacs (alveoli). (1)

(b) (i) Oxygen moves from the lungs into the bloodstream.

(ii) Carbon dioxide moves from the bloodstream into the lungs. (1)

2.19 It is the *proportions* of carbon dioxide and oxygen which change, whilst the nitrogen content, which plays no part in respiration, remains the same. (2)

2.20 Nicotine: damages blood vessels leading to increase of blood pressure and risk of heart disease. It also causes addiction. (2)

Tar: causes lung cancer and blocks the action of cilia that sweep away dust and microbes. (2)

Carbon monoxide: reduces supply of oxygen to the cells and contributes to disease of the heart and arteries. (2)

2.21 (a) Very overweight, largely because of excess fat in the body. (2)

(b) A combination of over-eating fatty and sugary foods, together with very little exercise. (2)

(c) More energy is required to move heavy parts of the body, so more work has to be done by the heart to pump the extra blood to the cells to achieve this. Extra weight can cause damage to joints. (2)

2.22 Bacteria live outside cells so can be killed by antibiotics. Viruses invade cells, so cannot be destroyed without causing damage to the cells. (2)

2.23 512 (the number doubles every 20 minutes). (2)

2.24 (i) Barriers such as skin, ear wax, tears. (1)

(ii) White blood cells. (1)

(iii) Blood clots that seal open wounds. (1)

2.25

light energy

$\boxed{\textbf{carbon dioxide + water}} \rightarrow \boxed{\textbf{glucose + oxygen}}$ (3)

chlorophyll

2.26 (a) Chlorophyll. (1)

(b) Green. (1)

(c) In the chloroplasts located in the cytoplasm of nearly every leaf and stem cell. (1)

(d) In the root, as photosynthesis cannot happen underground where there is no light. (1)

2.27 (a) Iodine solution. (1)

(b) The brown liquid turns blue/black if starch is present. (1)

(c) In good light (daytime), glucose is made at a faster rate than that at which it can be transported away, so this excess glucose is changed into starch. (1)

2.28 They are placed in different kingdoms because of the way they feed. Grass will make its own supply of sugar for respiration by photosynthesis, so it will be placed in the Plant Kingdom. Rabbits will eat and digest grass using the resulting sugar for respiration, so they will be placed in the Animal Kingdom. Mushrooms obtain their energy from the remains of dead organisms in the soil. They have no chloroplasts and do not carry out photosynthesis, so they will be placed in the Fungi Kingdom. (3)

2.29 These are discontinuous variations and they result from a combination of inherited genes and the environment i.e. lifestyle in terms of food intake and exercise. (2)

2.30 (a) They are both arthropods with the following features:
jointed limbs in pairs;
hard outer covering (exoskeleton);
bodies divided into segments (compartments). (2)

(b) (2)

Insects	Spiders
3 body parts	2 body parts
head; thorax; abdomen	head/thorax; abdomen
6 legs (3 pairs)	8 legs (4 pairs)
antennae	no antennae
usually 2 pairs of wings	no wings

2.31 The newt has a moist smooth skin; the lizard has a dry scaly skin. The newt lays eggs in water; the lizard lays shelled eggs on land. (3)

2.32 (a) Any three from: amount of water; light; temperature; pH(acidity/alkalinity); wind. (3)

(b) Any one from: predators/prey; competitors. (1)

2.33 (a) They will **increase** due to
(i) birth of new individuals;
(ii) individuals moving in (**immigration**) (2)

(b) They will **decrease** due to
(i) death of individuals;
(ii) individuals moving out (**emigration**) (2)

2.34 (a) algae / pond snail / leech / dragonfly nymph (1)

(b) algae / pond snail / leech / dragonfly nymph (1)

(c) lettuce / rabbit / fox / flea (1)

(d) grass / earthworm / shrew / owl (1)

(e) oak tree / aphid / ladybird / robin (1)

(f) lettuce / rabbit / fox / flea (1)

2.35 (a) When a body dies, the dead body is broken down into simple chemicals, such as nitrates, that enrich the soil. (1)

(b) Decomposers such as bacteria and fungi. (1)

(c) Enriched soil enables plants (primary producers) to grow, thrive and support the food web. (2)

Chapter 3 (11+ Chemistry)

3.1 (a) Flexibility: e.g. fabrics and metal wire. (2)

(b) Conductivity: e.g. all metals. (2)

(c) Hardness: e.g. diamond, steel tools and plastic safety helmets. (2)

(d) Strength: e.g. concrete for buildings, steel and fibre glass for boats. (2)

3.2 Weathering. (1)

3.3 (a) Large particles with big spaces between them; good drainage, hardly ever become waterlogged. (1)

(b) Very small particles with tiny spaces between them; poor drainage, often becomes waterlogged. (1)

3.4 ● Solid: fixed mass, volume and shape.

● Liquid: fixed mass and volume but changes shape.

● Gas: fixed mass, but changes volume and shape. (6)

3.5 (a) Solids: (i) Held strongly and closely in fixed positions. (ii) Vibrations in their fixed positions. (2)

(b) Liquids: (i) Close together but free to move around each other. (ii) Constantly moving around each other and to other places as liquid flows. (2)

(c) Gases: (i) Far apart with no forces of attraction between them. (ii) Move quickly in all directions. (2)

3.6 (a) Melting. (1)

(b) Evaporation. (1)

(c) Freezing. (1)

(d) Condensation. (1)

3.7 Any two from:

● Substances do not change into other substances – no chemical reaction.

● May change state.

● Changes are temporary and may be reversed. (2)

3.8 (a) Boiling point is raised well above 100°C. (1)

(b) To stop wet roads becoming icy as salt water freezes well below 0°C. (2)

3.9 (a) Oxygen and water. (Both are required.) (2)

(b) Any three from: covering iron with a layer of oil, zinc (galvanising), paint, plastic or tin. (3)

(c) Changes a strong useful solid into a weak useless powder. (2)

3.10 (a) Coal, oil and (natural) gas. (3)

(b) Candle wax, oil and (natural) gas. (3)

(c) Oxygen and heat. (2)

(d) Causes pollution of the air by releasing ash (smoke) and gases (carbon dioxide – greenhouse gas and/or sulphur dioxide – acid rain) into the atmosphere. (2)

3.11 (a) Soluble: able to dissolve in a solvent to form a solution.
Insoluble: not able to dissolve in a solvent. (2)

(b) The sulphur remains as a yellow solid (usually floating on top of the mixture); the copper sulphate dissolves in water to form a blue solution. (2)

(c) (i) Sulphur; (ii) copper sulphate solution. (2)

3.12 The missing words are as follows:

(a) Solids; different. (2)

(b) Insoluble; liquids. (2)

(c) Sink. (1)

(d) Decanting. (1)

3.13 (a) Solvent. (1)

(b) Evaporated; solute. (2)

Chapter 4 (13+ Chemistry)

4.1

Elements		Compounds		Mixtures	
Carbon	(1)	Carbon dioxide	(1)	Air	(1)
Iron filings	(1)	Distilled water	(1)	Sea water	(1)
Magnesium	(1)	Sodium chloride	(1)	Crude oil	(1)
Oxygen	(1)	Iron sulphide	(1)	Dilute sulphuric acid	(1)

Metal element		Non-metal element		Compound	
Iron filings	(1)	Carbon	(1)	Copper sulphate	(1)
Magnesium	(1)	Oxygen	(1)	Water	(1)
Mercury	(1)	Sulphur	(1)	Zinc oxide	(1)
Sodium	(1)				

4.3 (a) Mercury: the only one of these metals that is a liquid at room temperature. (2)

(b) Sodium: the only one of these metals that reacts with oxygen to form a base that is soluble in water, producing an alkali. The other oxides are insoluble in water. (2)

(c) Copper oxide: the only one of these oxides which is a solid and a base that neutralises acids. The others are gases which dissolve in water to form acids. (2)

(d) Sulphur: the only one which does not conduct electricity. (2)

4.4 Heating: adding energy to a substance to raise its temperature. (1)

Chemical reaction: rearranging elements to form completely new substances. (1)

Reactant: the substance you start with before a chemical reaction. (1)

Decompose: the splitting up of the substance into products, caused by a chemical reaction. (1)

Products: the substances produced as a result of a chemical reaction. (1)

4.5 (a) There will be an increase in mass during the reation as reactants combine to form products. (2)

(b) For example:

| magnesium (s) + oxygen (g) | → | magnesium oxide (s) | (5)

Magnesium has combined with oxygen from the air during burning to form magnesium oxide which has more mass because of the extra oxygen which has combined with the magnesium.

4.6 (a) (i) A – nitrogen; (ii) B – oxygen. (1)

(b) Any one from: carbon dioxide, noble gases (argon, krypton, helium, neon). (1)

(c) (i) Water vapour. (1)

(ii) Either white anhydrous copper sulphate turns blue or blue cobalt chloride turns pink. (2)

Process	Nitrogen		Oxygen		Carbon dioxide	
Burning a fossil fuel	Same	(1)	Decrease	(1)	Increase	(1)
Photosynthesis	Same	(1)	Increase	(1)	Decrease	(1)
Respiration	Same	(1)	Decrease	(1)	Increase	(1)
Passing air through limewater	Same	(1)	Same	(1)	Decrease	(1)
Rusting	Same	(1)	Decrease	(1)	Same	(1)

4.8 (a) See diagram on page 84. (6)

    (b) See if it boils at 100 °C – if it does, it is pure. (2)

4.9 (a) Evaporation. (1)

    (b) Filtration. (1)

    (c) Chromatography. (1)

    (d) Fractional distillation. (1)

4.10 Hydrochloric acid – red. (1)

    Limewater – stays blue. (1)

    Sodium hydroxide – stays blue. (1)

    Sugar solution – stays blue. (1)

    Water – stays blue. (1)

4.11. pH scale (a scale of numbers ranging from 1 to 14).

1	2	3	4	5	6	7	8	9	10	11	12	13	14

Becoming more acidic   Weak acid   Neutral   Weak alkali   Becoming more alkali

(5)

4.12. (a) Salt. (1)

    (b) Salt. (1)

    (c) Carbon dioxide; salt (answers may be in either order). (2)

    (d) Hydrogen; salt (answers may be in either order). (2)

    (e) Lowers. (1)

    (f) Raises (increases). (1)

    (g) Does not change. (1)

4.13 A chemical reaction that involves combination with oxygen. (2)

4.14 (a) A compound that contains only the elements hydrogen and carbon. (1)

(b) Carbon dioxide and water. (2)

(c) Methane (g) + oxygen (g) → carbon dioxide (g) + water (g) + energy (heat and light). (4)

4.15 (a) Fuels formed from the dead remains of animals and plants that lived millions of years ago. (1)

(b) Oil and gas. (2)

(c) (i) Carbon dioxide and sulphur dioxide. (2)

(ii) Carbon dioxide dissolves to form a weak acid (carbonic acid) which is why rain is always slightly acid. (1)

Sulphur dioxide dissolves to form a strong acid (sulphuric acid) which is responsible for the acid rain that affects plant life and corrodes metals and buildings. (1)

4.16 (a) Rusting costs money (i) to replace items that have rusted, (ii) to take measures to prevent rusting from taking place. (2)

(b) Iron, oxygen and water. (3)

(c) (i) By covering the iron with a layer of grease, oil, paint or plastic. (1)

(ii) By covering the iron with a less reactive metal, e.g. tin. (1)

(iii) By coating iron with a layer of zinc (i.e. galvanising). This is known as sacrificial protection. (1)

4.17 Metals are placed in order according to how well they react with oxygen, water, steam and acids in what is called the reactivity series. (1)

4.18 Oxidation: combining with oxygen. (2)

Reduction: removal of oxygen from a compound by another substance. (2)

4.19 (a) zinc + magnesium oxide → no reaction (2)

(b) zinc + copper oxide → zinc oxide + copper (2)

(c) magnesium + iron oxide → magnesium oxide + iron (2)

(d) iron + copper sulphate → iron sulphate + copper (2)

(e) iron + magnesium sulphate → no reaction (2)

(f) zinc + iron sulphate → zinc sulphate + iron (2)

4.20 D, B, C, A (most reactive first). (4)

4.21 (a) (i) Copper oxide. (1)

(ii) copper oxide + carbon → carbon dioxide + copper (4)

(b) (i) Raise the pH. (1)

(ii) An iron nail. (1)

4.22 | iron oxide + carbon | → | iron + carbon dioxide | (4)

4.23 Iron is higher than copper in the reactivity series and is harder to extract, i.e. far greater temperatures than those produced by a charcoal fire are needed. Iron was only able to be extracted when the technology for creating more heat from better furnaces had been developed. (3)

4.24 (a) | galena (lead sulphide) + oxygen + heat | → | lead oxide + sulphur dioxide | (5)

(b) | lead oxide + carbon + heat | → | lead + carbon dioxide | (5)

(c) Yes. Iron is higher than lead in the reactivity series. (2)

4.25 (a) The blast is a blast of hot air which means a supply of oxygen. (2)

(b) Iron ore: the source of iron. (2)

Limestone: to produce carbon dioxide which helps make carbon monoxide (the main reducing agent) and to turn sandy rock into slag. (2)

Coke: a supply of carbon to combine with carbon dioxide to make carbon monoxide. (2)

(c) Carbon monoxide. (1)

(d) | iron oxide + carbon monoxide | → | iron + carbon dioxide | (4)

(e) Molten iron and molten slag. (2)

4.26 (a) Gold, iron, aluminium. (3)

(b) Aluminium requires large quantities of electricity to extract it from its ore. This, and the high temperatures required, make it a much more expensive process than the extraction of iron. (2)

(c) Gold is a rare metal, found in small quantities. (2)

Chapter 5 (11+ Physics)

5.1 (a) Normal brightness. (1)

(b) Bright. (1)

(c) Dim. (1)

5.2 (a)

(3)

(b) They will be equally dim. (1)

(c) (i) There is a gap in the circuit. (1)

(ii) One/more of the lamps might be broken. (1)

(iii) One of the cells is the wrong way round. (1)

5.3 Current always takes the easiest route which may not always be the shortest route. (2)

5.4 Any four from:

- Make a stationary object move.

- Make a moving object go faster or slower.

- Make a moving object change direction.

- Make a moving object stop.

- Change the shape of an object. (4)

5.5 Weight of the boat (downwards); upthrust by water (upwards). (2)

5.6 When a force acts, the other force of the pair acting in the opposite direction is called the reaction force. (1)

5.7 (a) Materials that are attracted by a magnet are said to be magnetic. (1)

(b) The end of a magnet that points towards the geographical north pole is called the north-seeking pole. (1)

(c) Unlike poles attract; like poles repel. (2)

5.8 (a) Weight. (1)

(b) Downwards towards the Earth's centre. (1)

5.9 (a) A force that opposes motion. (1)

(b) When two substances rub together. (1)

5.10 Any four from:

- Tyres and road: useful for grip, movement and control of direction – help.

- Shape of cyclist: air resistance slows movement, so speed cyclists will crouch to be as streamlined as possible – nuisance.

- Gears and chain: friction adds to the effort needed to turn these – nuisance.

- Brakes: enable the cycle to be stopped – help.

- Rubber on handlebar grips: make it easier to hold on – help. (8)

5.11 Light from a luminous source reflects off the table into our eyes. (2)

5.12 (a) Transparent. (1)

(b) Opaque. (1)

(c) Translucent. (1)

5.13 It bounces off the surface at the same angle as it hits the mirror surface. This is called reflection. (2)

5.14 By vibrations. (2)

5.15 (a) Pluck it to start it vibrating. (2)

(b) Tighten the string or make it shorter. (2)

(c) Pluck it harder to make bigger vibrations. (1)

5.16 Space is said to be a vacuum and sound is not able to travel through a vacuum because there are no particles to squash or stretch. (2)

5.17 The Earth spins on its axis, completing one turn every 24 hours. During this time, half of the Earth faces the Sun – daytime – whilst the other half is in darkness – night-time. (1)

5.18 The spinning of the Earth. (1)

5.19 Midday – Sun is high in the sky and shadows are shortest. (1)

Evening – Sun is low in the sky and shadows are long. (1)

5.20 28 days – this is the time it takes for the Moon to orbit the Earth. (2)

5.21 The Moon is not a light source and it is hard to see during daytime. We see it best at night because light from the Sun is reflected from it. (2)

Chapter 6 (13+ Physics)

6.1 Mass and volume. (2)

6.2 Density = mass/volume. (3)

6.3 (a) A = 7.5 g/cm³. (2)

(b) B = 11.0 g/cm³. (2)

(c) C = 2.7 g/cm³. (2)

(d) D = 2.7 g/cm³. (2)

6.4 C and D are the same material. They have the same density. (2)

6.5 Glass (volume 1071 cm³; volume of marble 937 cm³). (1)

6.6 234 000 g or 234 kg. (2)

6.7 (a)

(4)

(b) The ammeter reading goes down. (1)

(c) It must be connected the right way round, i.e. positive to positive. (1)

6.8 (a) (i) A; (ii) A and B. (2)

(b) (i) A and B; (ii) A and C. (2)

6.9 (a) No. Once a fuse 'blows', the circuit is broken immediately, so the second fuse is not needed. (2)

(b) When there is a current in a circuit which is too high for the fuse, the fuse wire heats, melts and breaks the circuit, stopping all current in the circuit immediately. (2)

(c) To protect components from currents which are too large and might well damage them. (2)

6.10 (a) Wrap the insulated wire around the iron nail and connect each end of the wire to a battery or cell. (3)

(b) Bring a magnet close to the nail. If there is repulsion between the two, then the nail has become a magnet. (2)

(c) Either increase the number of turns of wire or increase the current by adding another battery or more cells. (2)

6.11 (a) An AND circuit. (1)

(b)

Inputs		Output
A	B	Q
0	0	0
0	1	0
1	0	0
1	1	1

(9)

6.12 (a) 30 N. (2)

(b) 300 N. (2)

(c) 1800 N. (2)

(d) 5 N. (2)

(e) 3.2 N. (2)

6.13 (a) 40 kg. (2)

(b) 400 N. (2)

(c) 64 N. (2)

6.14 (a) Increase; accelerate. (2)

(b) Decrease. (1)

(c) Constant speed. (1)

6.15 (a) 48 cm. (2)

(b) 4 cm. (2)

179

6.16 45 Nm (TM = 300 N x 0.15 m).   (2)

6.17 10 N.   (2)

6.18 360 cm away from the pivot.   (2)

6.19 (a) 6 N/cm².   (2)

    (b) 5 N/cm².   (2)

    (c) 1000 N/cm².   (2)

6.20 4 cm².   (2)

6.21 Any three from:

    ● They are very fast.

    ● They travel in straight lines.

    ● They will not travel through opaque materials, so forming shadows.

    ● They can be absorbed.   (3)

6.22 (a) The bending of a light ray.   (1)

    (b) At the boundary between two different materials through which a light ray is
        passing.   (1)

    (c) Light changes speed as it passes through materials that have different densities.   (1)

6.23 (a)

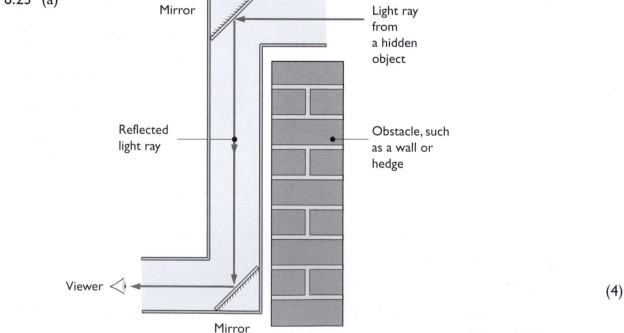

                                                  (4)

    (b) A periscope.   (1)

6.24 3000 m or 3 km.   (2)

6.25 3.3 s.   (2)

6.26 (a) (i) Frequency; (ii) amplitude. (2)

(b) The high, loud note has higher frequency and larger amplitude than the low, quiet note. (2)

6.27 The Earth is tilted on its axis, making part of it closer to the Sun. (2)

6.28 (a) Earth; Sun. (2)

(b) Moon; Earth. (2)

6.29 The distance that light travels in one year. (1)

6.30 Because light from the stars does not have to pass though the Earth's atmosphere which would absorb some of the light, reducing the quality of the pictures. (2)

6.31 (a) Work is done when (i) a force produces motion; (ii) when something is heated. (1)

(b) Joules (J). (1)

(c) Amount of work done (J) = amount of energy supplied (J). (2)

6.32 When energy changes form:

total amount of energy at the start = total amount of energy at the end (2)

6.33

Form of energy at start		Transducer		Form(s) of energy at end	
Electrical		Lamp	(1)	Heat, light	(1)
Chemical	(1)	Cell		Electrical, heat	
Chemical		Bunsen burner		Heat, light, sound	(3)
Sound		Microphone		Electrical, heat	(1)
Electrical	(1)	Loudspeaker		Sound, heat	
Electrical		Motor		Kinetic, sound, heat	(1)
Kinetic	(1)	Dynamo/generator		Electrical, sound, heat	
Light		Solar cell	(1)	Electrical, heat	

6.34 (a) Fuels formed from the fossilised remains of animals and plants that lived over many millions of years ago. (2)

(b) Any two from: coal, oil and gas. (2)

(c) Once burned, they cannot be used again and we are using them up faster than they can be replaced (if at all). (2)

(d) No. Fossil fuels provide raw materials for the manufacture of plastics, medicines, cosmetics and synthetic fibres. (2)

6.35 (a) Light and heat. (2)

(b) Heat. (1)

6.36

$$\boxed{\text{Gravitational potential energy}}$$
$$\blacktriangledown$$
$$\boxed{\text{kinetic energy}}$$
$$\blacktriangledown$$
$$\boxed{\text{electrical energy + sound energy + light energy + heat}}$$

(6)

6.37 The cup of tea cools to room temperature (20 °C). The tea, now at 20 °C, is put into your mouth which is at 37 °C. Heat will flow out from your mouth to the tea, so the tea will feel cold.

(3)

Test yourself answers

Chapter 1 (11+ Biology)

1.   Any living thing.

2.   (a) Nutrition, movement, reproduction, growth.

     (b) Nutrition: obtain and absorb food.

         Movement: change of place and/or position.

         Reproduction: an organism making more of its own kind.

         Growth: becoming bigger by increasing size and/or number of cells.

3.   (a) Pumps blood around the body.

     (b) Takes blood away from the heart to the body.

     (c) Takes blood towards the heart from the body.

4.   Any two from: jointed limbs (in pairs); hard outer bodies (exoskeleton); segmented bodies.

5.   (a) The place where an organism lives.

     (b) The sum of all biological (e.g. other animals and plants), chemical (e.g. pH, salinity of water) and physical (e.g. light, temperature) factors that affect an organism.

Chapter 2 (13+ Biology)

1.   **Animal cell**   **Plant cell**

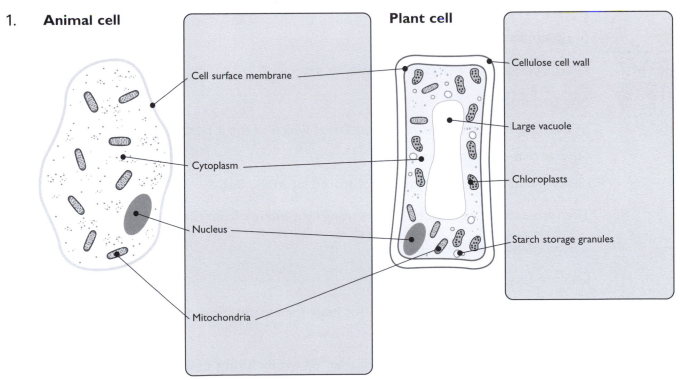

2. Tissue: specialised cells of the same type combined together, e.g. muscles, skin layers.

   Organ: a structure made from various tissues that performs a specific function, e.g. eye, leaf, carpel.

   System: a collection of combined organs that enable a specific job to be done, e.g. reproductive system.

3. (a) (i) Carbohydrate (although fats provide a storage of energy for use when supplies of carbohydrate become low).

   (ii) Sugar – fruits, jams, sweets, soft drinks; starch – potatoes, flour products, nuts.

   (b) (i) Protein.

   (ii) Meats, fish, milk, cheese, eggs, nuts.

4. (i) Chemicals made of protein that enable chemical reactions to happen.

   (ii) Remain unchanged as they work.

   (iii) There is a different enzyme for each reaction in the body.

5. (a) A non-elastic thread that attaches muscle to bone.

   (b) A thread that joins bone to bone at a joint. This is elastic enough to allow movement.

6. (a) Puberty.

   (b) Sperm cell; testis or testes.

   (c) Egg cell or ovum; ovary or ovaries.

   (d) Zygote.

   (e) Implantation.

   (f) Pregnant.

7. Mouth; trachea; bronchus; bronchiole; air sac.

8. Any two from:

   (i) Exercise causes the heart to beat faster which keeps it healthy.

   (ii) Exercise develops muscles.

   (iii) Exercise reduces the amount of stored fat in the body.

9. The manufacture of food by a plant using light energy from the Sun.

10. Carbon dioxide and water.

11. Glucose (sugar) and oxygen.

12. Some of this will be used by the plant itself, for **respiration**. Oxygen not used by the plant will be released through the **stomata**.

13. It is used for respiration which is needed by **every living cell**. The leaves make more glucose than they need, so glucose is transported to other parts of the plant for respiration by a process called **translocation**.

It is also used for making living material – increasing biomass.

In order to grow, plants need a constant supply of proteins, chlorophyll and fats which can be made from sugars such as glucose.

14. (a) As soluble salts dissolved in the water in the soil around the plants roots.

(b) Numerous thin-walled root hair cells which absorb water and soluble salts.

The great number of root hair cells increases **surface area** and the **thin cell walls** enable water and minerals to be taken into the plant more efficiently.

15. The differences between organisms of the same species.

16. Any one from: colour of eyes/hair; blood group; male/female; freckles or the shape of the face. These are features which result from the inheritance of genes from the parents.

17. Sorting organisms with similar characteristics (features) into groups.

18. Both are vertebrates and belong to the class Mammals. Both are warm-blooded, have skins which are partially covered with hair or fur. Both will have been born alive and fed on milk from the mother's mammary gland.

19. Jointed limbs in pairs; hard outer covering (exoskeleton); bodies divided into segments (compartments).

20.

Vertebrate	Invertebrate
emu	earthworm
shark	spider
whale	crab
frog	beetle
turtle	
fox	

21. (i) The place where a living organism lives is called its **habitat**. Examples of habitats include a pond, a field, a hedgerow, a wood, your house.

(ii) This refers to **all of the living organisms** within a habitat. The community will consist of a collection of **populations**.

22. An ecosystem is a habitat (the place) and the communities (populations of living organisms) added together.

23. The word describes the conditions within an ecosystem.

24. This refers to the numbers of organisms of the **same species**, which exist in a habitat.

25. Food shortage; shortage of space; increase of toxins (poisons); predation.

26. (a) Rose. It is the only organism in the chain which can make its own food – using photosynthesis. It is the primary source of food in the chain.

(b) Any two from:
Aphids die out – killed by insecticide
Rose grows better – not being eaten by aphids
Robin and cat might move away – a supply of food has disappeared.

27. (a) A food web is a set of interconnected food chains.

(b) In a food web, consumers have more than one supply of food, unlike a food chain, where there is only one supply of food.

Chapter 3 (11+ Chemistry)

1. (a) These are special to substances and may be observed and/or measured without the substances changing into another substance.

(b) The composition of a substance and how it changes into another substance. When this happens, a chemical reaction has taken place.

2. Decayed animal and plant remains that add nutrients and help keep soil moist.

3. (a) C – solid.

(b) B – liquid.

(c) A – gas.

4. ● New substances are made as a result of a chemical reaction.

● Change is permanent and cannot be reversed.

5. (a) Ink.

(b) Water.

(c) Blue powder.

Chapter 4 (13+ Chemistry)

1. (a) A single substance which forms the building blocks of all matter.

(b) 100

(c) In the Periodic Table.

(d) The atoms of any particular element are all the same.

2. (a) Negatively charged particles which move around the nucleus of an atom.

(b) Particles found within the nucleus of an atom that have mass, but no electric charge.

(c) Positively charged particles found within the nucleus of an atom.

3. All elements present as reactants will also be present in the product(s) of a chemical reaction.

    The total mass of reactant(s) = the total mass of product(s).

4. (a) Changes in appearance to indicate the presence of particular substances.

    (b) Any four from:

    - Limewater: to test for presence of carbon dioxide.
    - Anhydrous copper sulphate: to test for presence of water.
    - Anhydrous cobalt chloride: to test for presence of water.
    - Litmus: to test for presence of acids/alkalis.
    - Universal indicator: to test for the presence and strength of acids/alkalis.

5. (a) Hydrochloric acid: stays red.

    (b) Limewater: turns blue.

    (c) Sodium hydroxide: turns blue.

    (d) Sugar solution: stays red.

    (e) Water: stays red.

6. Oxygen is the only colourless gas that re-lights a glowing splint.

7. (a) | carbon (s) + oxygen (g) | → | carbon dioxide (g) |

    (b) | magnesium (s) + oxygen (g) | → | magnesium oxide (s) |

    (c) | sulphur (s) + oxygen (g) | → | sulphur dioxide (g) |

8. (a) | copper sulphate + iron | → | iron sulphate + copper |

    (b) | silver nitrate + copper | → | copper nitrate + silver |

9. A substance that is a mixture of a metal compound and rock.

10. (a) Plastic: light and does not break.

    (b) Copper: a very good conductor of electricity; flexible as thin wires.

    (c) Plastic: easy to shape and does not rust; does not need painting regularly.

    (d) Iron: strong and will not melt at the temperature of hot ash.

    (e) Aluminium: strong and light (low density).

Chapter 5 (11+ Physics)

1.

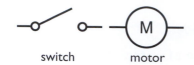

2. Components are connected together one after the other in a single path.

3. A push or pull.

4. Newtons (N).

5. A newton meter (newton spring balance).

6   A force of attraction between any two bodies.

7. Push – gravity only pulls.

8. Any three from: Sun, stars, lamps, television sets, flames.

9. Light travels in straight lines.

    Light travels very fast.

10. (a) 365¼ days.

    (b) One year.

11. A moon orbits a planet. A planet orbits a star.

Chapter 6 (13+ Physics)

1. (a) A ruler marked in cm.

    (b) A balance (scales) marked in g.

    (c) A ruler marked in cm. Measure lengths and multiply to find volume in cm^3.

    (d) A measuring cylinder marked in cm^3. Pour water from water bottle into the cylinder and read off the volume.

    (e) A measuring cylinder with some water in it. Measure the volume of water that the keys displace in cm^3.

2. 9000

3. 30 000 g (or 30 kg).

4.

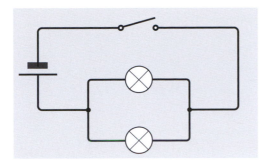

5. Weight (N) = mass (kg) x gravitational force (N/kg).

6. (a) 7 cm.

   (b) 7.5 cm.

7. ● A rigid body.

   ● Able to turn about a pivot.

8. (a) Incident ray.

   (b) It bounces off at the same angle.

   (c) Reflection.

9.

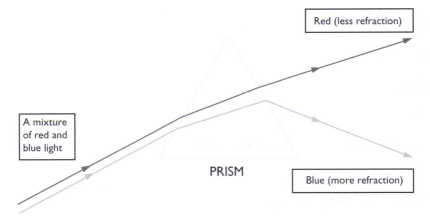

10.

	Height of Sun	Temperature of Earth's surface	Length of shadow	Length of day
Summer	High	Warm	Short	Long
Winter	Low	Cold	Long	Short

11. Planet; star; Solar System; galaxy; universe.

12. Energy is a measure of (i) work that has been done or (ii) work that is able to be done.

13.   Any five from:

- Kinetic energy.

- Gravitational potential energy.

- Elastic (strain) energy.

- Chemical energy.

- Electrical energy.

- Thermal energy.

- Light energy.

- Sound energy.

- Nuclear energy.

  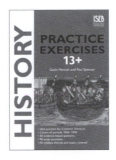  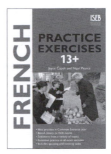

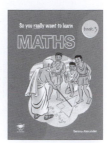

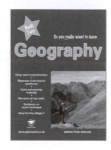